Meals-in-a-Jar
Made Easy

40 SHELF STABLE RECIPES USING FREEZE-DRIED FOODS

by Jodi Weiss Schroeder

ISBN: 9798364169501

To my sweet husband and seven kids,
the taste-testers for all my recipes.

TABLE OF CONTENTS

FOREWORD

As a long-time friend and fan of Jodi Weiss Schroeder, I am thrilled to write the foreword for this book. As soon as she mentioned she was working on this new project, I asked if I could write the foreword – that's how confident I am in Jodi's knowledge and how much I appreciate her devotion to helping families.

With Jodi's large and busy family, life is hectic and serving up the meals to keep her family happy can be challenging, but if anyone can meet that challenge, it's her! She has been on the forefront of creating quick, nutritious, and delicious meals using freeze-dried foods. Inside this book you'll find the results of Jodi's hands-on experience. She shares honest stories from the heart of her growing family and how she developed a clever system of utilizing freeze-dried and dehydrated foods in recipes that can be assembled and stored in mason jars for future meals.

As someone who has been on the receiving end of Jodi's advice and guidance, I can attest to the value of her knowledge and expertise. The information in this book is clear, concise, and easy to understand. You'll know exactly how to assemble and prepare her simple, delicious recipes and she even gives shopping lists for making them in bulk.

This is the type of book that becomes worn and food-stained over the years as you refer to it again and again. Whether you are new to the concept of freeze-dried food and food storage, or you are looking for new ideas and strategies for simpler mealtimes, this book will provide valuable insights and inspiration.

I am grateful to Jodi for generously sharing her expertise, and can't wait to treat my own family to some of her delicious recipes!

Lisa Bedford
~The Survival Mom

Lisa Bedford and Jodi Weiss Schroeder

Nothing brings people together like good food

INTRODUCTION

Welcome to my Meals-in-a-Jar Made Easy cookbook. I'm Jodi and I have been teaching people about long term food storage, survivalism, and emergency preparedness on my blog Food Storage Made Easy (http://foodstoragemadeeasy.net) since 2009. I started the blog with my sister-in-law Julie when we were just two young moms trying to learn how to build up a supply of food that our kids would actually eat and sharing what we learned along the way. We didn't know if we would ever need to use it, but we wanted to be prepared, just in case.

We started learning the basics of how to cook with foods that have a long shelf life such as wheat, beans, and rice. We ventured into using powdered milk and dried eggs, then even practiced cooking without power because who knows when you might have a powerless emergency and still have children demanding dinner. We created a food storage calculator to help us figure out how much to store for a year's worth of food. However, as I started looked at the buckets of dried goods in my basement, I panicked realizing I didn't actually know what I would cook for a year with those ingredients. I started trying to meal plan based on these foods but was coming up short on ideas.

As I built my food storage in baby steps, I started adding a lot of freeze-dried fruits, vegetables, and meats to my supplies. I figured they would be a great supplement to the basics that I already had. We were always taught to store what you eat and eat what you store. I refuse to have anything in my food storage that I don't know how to use, so I started cooking with freeze-dried foods and I fell *in love*! Not only was I rotating through my prepared meals but I was saving time (and even money) in the kitchen on a regular basis. Instead of keeping all the food in the basement, I made space in my kitchen pantry to store one of each item so I could use it daily. My kids love to snack on the fruit and yogurt, I never chop onions any more, and I can whip up dinner in 15-20 minutes any night of the week!

As I started cooking more with freeze-dried foods, I realized I could make entire meals using all shelf-stable items and could start to plan my emergency meals around that. While it wasn't difficult for me to come up with breakfast and lunch ideas using basic food storage ingredients, dinner was where I struggled in my long term food storage menu planning. I decided if I could invent delicious normal meals using freeze-dried items it would solve my meal-planning dilemma. I tried to figure out the most cost-effective way to do this and how best to store these meals I was creating. I had seen some jar meals on Pinterest (http://pinterest.com/fsme) and thought that they might be a great option for this project. I started experimenting by making a few complete meals that I could store on the shelf and just add water when it was time to cook. I was quickly sold!

In order to save money, I started creating recipes based off of the monthly specials at Thrive Life because I was already stocking up each month on those sale items. I would make batches of 10 jars of the same recipe, greatly reducing the cost per jar. Just think, by doing this every month you could have 120 extra meals prepped within a year! Do that for a few years and you would have enough meals for a delicious, normal dinner every night should an emergency arise and you needed to live off of your food storage for a whole year. The key to this strategy is to make sure to rotate through the meals or you won't enjoy them very much when it comes time to eat them.

Fast forward a few years to 2015 -- I went through a pretty rough divorce and became a single mama to four precious kids (you may have seen pics and videos of them if you've followed our blog over the years). I found myself needing a full-time income and my partner Julie had a lot of family changes happening so she didn't have as much time to work on the blog anymore. I took over and started running the blog, sending out the monthly email newsletters, and moderating our popular Facebook group (http://facebook.com/groups/foodstoragemadeeasy) on my own. I still had to work a few other part-time jobs to make ends meet and life became busier than ever. Suddenly, I had to run kids to soccer, practice piano with them, do all the school drives and choir car pools, teach piano lessons and do marketing consulting work, while still keep up with Food Storage Made Easy AND get dinner on the table every night. Fast food wasn't an option because it was expensive and I didn't even have time to run to a restaurant on some nights.

One busy night, I was feeling deflated and defeated. I was tired of giving my kids unhealthy quick and easy staples like ramen and mac and cheese for dinner. My 12-year-old son offered to cook something because I literally had zero time to cook and everyone was starving. I had just finished a batch of jar meals and asked him if he wanted to try making one of those. He was up for the challenge and made a yummy meal in just 10 minutes while I was running the other kids in different directions. Dinner was saved!

My little chef, Mikey

The moral of this long story is that while meals-in-a-jar can be great for emergency preparedness meal planning and building a year supply of normal meals that your family will love, they are also *perfect* for busy families with busy lives. I also love to give them as gifts or to help families in need. I've even started putting them into my 72 hour kits. Don't be afraid of being called one of those "crazy preppers" for cooking this way. Instead, have confidence in knowing that you are about to become a meal magician!

Today I'm an even busier mom of ***seven*** since adding a new husband and three bonus kids to my crew. With five teenagers in one house I find myself using two jar meals to feed the whole family some days. The good news is that it's still faster, healthier, and even *cheaper* than making a McDonalds run on a busy night! I hope you enjoy this new way of cooking whether you are using it to prepare for life's big emergencies, like a pandemic or a natural disaster, or for life's little emergencies like starving kids on a busy night.

MEALS-IN-A-JAR BASICS

What is a meal-in-a-jar?
A meal-in-a-jar recipe is composed of mainly freeze-dried or dehydrated ingredients, typically with simple cooking instructions like "just-add-water" and "cook for 10 minutes". Since these jar meals use shelf stable ingredients with a long shelf life they are great to make up in batches to save for a rainy (or busy) day. Here are a few of the ways you can use these amazing meals:

- Long term food storage already organized into meals
- "Fast food" on busy nights
- Holiday neighbor gifts or teacher appreciation gifts
- Meals for those in need (sick, new parents, etc.)
- Church or group activity (make lots of jars and each person can take a few home)
- Alternative for freezer meals
- Backpacking/hiking meals (if stored in mylar pouches)
- 72 hour kit meals (cut the recipes in half or quarters to make single servings)

Tips for buying ingredients:
I have created these recipes based mainly on freeze-dried foods because they have a long shelf life and take less water, time, and fuel to prepare. Dehydrated foods may be substituted if you don't have access to freeze-dried foods or need a cheaper alternative. However, if you make substitutions, water amounts and cook times may need to be adjusted.

Many ingredients can be substituted with ease. You can use whatever meat you have on hand or that is on sale that month. Fruits and veggies can be substituted based on preference or sales. For example, a recipe may call for onion slices but you can use chopped onions instead. Also, most recipes calling for flour or pasta can use gluten-free substitutions.

Home freeze-dried foods can be a great alternative if you have access to a Harvest Right Freeze-Dryer. If you are interested in buying a home freeze-dryer, visit my affiliate link at https://affiliates.harvestright.com/132.html and I will get a small thank-you check from them.

Tips for filling your jars:
"Pretty Method": If you want your jars to look uniform and pretty (for gifts), fill the jars with items from smallest to largest. This is the order I have listed in each of the recipes. Gently twist the jar to get items to settle or pack down each layer with a spoon to fit a little bit more. Each recipe was created to be able to fit into one jar, but if you scoop a little bit heavier on any items you may end up needing to use a little bit less of the bigger items to get everything to fit.

"Filling Method": If you want to pack your jars as full as possible, place your larger items at the bottom and periodically shake up the jar to mix everything all together. This should allow you to use heaping scoops of each ingredient. You can boost your number of servings by getting up to 1/2 cup or more of extra food into a jar. If you have a larger family or hungry teenage boys this can be a good option. Water amounts may need to be slightly adjusted using this method.

Tips for sealing your jars:

To extend the shelf life of your jar meals, I recommend using a jar lid attachment for a vacuum sealer. The vacuum sealer brand I like best is FoodSaver. If you don't already have a FoodSaver machine you can buy an inexpensive jar lid kit that includes a manual pump on Amazon. You can view the exact one I bought here: ***https://amzn.to/3Fmd6CH***

To seal your jar, place two canning lids on top of the jar. They don't need to be new but they should not be warped or visibly damaged. Place the jar sealer attachment over the top and press "seal" on your vacuum sealer. You will hear a release when it is finished. Pull off the attachment and the top jar lid. The bottom lid should be securely attached to the jar and all of the oxygen removed. You can place a canning ring over top and store it in the pantry.

You can also use oxygen absorbers to extend the shelf life of your jar meals, but I find this method to be slightly more inconvenient. They take up extra space in your jar and it's more expensive to keep buying new ones for each use. If you do choose to use oxygen absorbers, use the 200cc size for quart jars. Place one absorber in the top of the jar and top tightly with a canning lid and ring.Your lid should seal within a few hours. Oxygen absorbers are available on Amazon. These are some of the ones that I've purchased in the past: ***https://amzn.to/3BnI3Ea***

If you are planning to use these meals for backpacking, 72 hour kits, or to send in the mail, you can also store them in mylar bags with an oxygen absorber. This is also a good option if you need to make double recipes like me!

What is the shelf life of meals-in-a-jar?

The shelf life of most of the recipes in this book will be approximately 1 year because that is the shelf life of most freeze-dried foods once their initial container has been opened. Storing your jars in a cool, dark location with the oxygen properly removed can extend the shelf life to 4-5 years or even longer as light, heat, and oxygen are the biggest enemies to shelf life.

What's included with each recipe?

Each of the 40+ recipes in this book contain a list of ingredients you will need to make the meal. Recipes call for freeze-dried (FD) foods, dehydrated foods, powders, sauce mixes, etc. I will provide tips on where I like to purchase my foods in the next chapter. You'll get any specific instructions on how to fill the jar along with instructions on how to prepare the meal when you are ready to cook it. There is also a shopping list to help you put together a bulk batch of that recipe, which is the most cost-effective way to do it. Each bulk batch will usually make 10-11 meals that can be stored for later. There is also an example label for each recipe. Complete label sheets for each recipe can be downloaded at ***http://bit.ly/MIJ-labels***

FREEZE-DRIED FOODS

As I mentioned above, most of the recipes here are based on freeze-dried foods. In addition to their long shelf life and ease of use, they are also the closest equivalent to cooking with fresh food when compared to other preserved foods. Here are a few considerations when you are deciding whether to substitute freeze-dried ingredients with dehydrated in these recipes.

What is Dehydrating?

Dehydrating is a very old method of food preservation. Modern dehydration involves heating up the food by circulating warm air over it that is hot enough to remove the moisture but not hot enough to cook the food. This ends up with a shriveled and denser version of the original food (think of a raisin). When hydrated, they do not return fully to their original form, but will plump up as they accept moisture back in. Most dehydrated foods are preserved with some sort of additives in order to extend shelf life.

What is Freeze-Drying?

Freeze-drying is a process that allows food to be shelf stable while retaining the maximum amount of nutrients. Freeze-dried foods keep their original color, form, size, taste and texture.

The freeze-drying process has four steps:
1. **FLASH FREEZE:** Foods are flash-frozen within hours of being picked. This allows them to be picked at peak ripeness. unlike grocery store foods that have been sitting on trucks for weeks.
2. **VAPORIZE:** In a vacuum chamber, 98% of the moisture is removed by vaporizing the ice at -50 degrees. Removing the moisture is what allows the foods to be preserved for a long time.
3. **SEAL**: The food is sealed in moisture-proof / oxygen-proof cans to ensure freshness.
4: **ENJOY:** When the water is replaced, the foods regain their original fresh flavor, aroma, nutrients, texture and appearance, making them perfect for everyday cooking and snacking. The long shelf life makes them wonderful for long term food storage as well.

Freeze-Dried Bell Peppers
Dehydrated Bell Peppers

Dehydrated vs Freeze-Dried Comparison

Moisture Content:
Freeze-Dried = lower (1-2% retained)
Dehydrated = higher (5-10% retained)

Shelf Life:
Freeze-Dried = longer (20-25 years)
Dehydrated = shorter (7-10 years)

Weight:
Freeze-Dried = lighter
Dehydrated = heavier

Storage Needed per Fresh Equivalent:
Freeze-Dried = bigger
Dehydrated = smaller

Nutrients Retained:
Freeze-Dried = more
Dehydrated = less

Preservatives Typically Added:
Freeze-Dried = no
Dehydrated = yes

Natural Shape /Size Retained After Hydration:
Freeze-Dried = yes
Dehydrated = no

Ease of Preparation/Cooking:
Freeze-Dried = fast to hydrate, easy, pre-cooked
Dehydrated = slower, more water needed

Uses:
Freeze Dried = Stir fries, omelets, fresh
Dehydrated = soups, stews, casseroles

Cost:
Freeze Dried = more expensive
Dehydrated = less expensive

RECOMMENDED FOOD BRAND: THRIVE LIFE

I have tried most of the commercial available brands of freeze-dried foods and also food that I have freeze-dried and dehydrated on my own. Hands down I have found **Thrive Life** to have the highest quality, best-tasting foods across the board and they are the most allergen-friendly. Here are some additional reasons they are my recommended brand:

Source: Thrive can pick the very best suppliers of raw ingredients since they freeze-dry all items at their factory in Utah. They won't accept products sourced from China, or anywhere else that can't guarantee high quality standards. Foods are sourced within the USA whenever possible!
Taste & Appearance: Every new product goes through several phases of testing by the R&D department, culinary team, and outside groups to make sure it looks and tastes great.
Quality: All foods must go through Thrive's proprietary **NutriLock Process** which utilizes a 40+ step process to ensure every product is the highest quality. All products are inspected and tested for microbiological contaminants, bacteria, pesticides, and food safety.
Health: Thrive Life makes sure all new products are non-GMO, have no MSG, and contain no hydrogenated oils, preservatives, or artificial flavors or colors whenever possible.

Shop With Me:

I became a Thrive Life consultant to help my blog readers get the best prices on food and to make sure they know about sales. I do cooking demos featuring the foods that are on sale every month. Many of the recipes in this book were based around what items were on sale in the month I developed it. **Join my Thrive Email List** to get all these benefits and other bonuses for shopping with me! Visit this link to sign up: *https://yourthrivelife.com/join-my-thrive-list/*

"There has never been a sadness that can't been cured by breakfast food."
—Ron Swanson

BREAKFAST FOODS

Eggs in a Jar

Eggs in a Jar

Bulk Batch Shopping List

Makes 25 half-pint jars

Dried Egg Powder (1 #10 can)
FD Chopped Onions (1 pantry can)
FD Green Bell Peppers (1 pantry can)
FD Mushrooms (1 pantry can)
FD Sausage Crumbles (1 pantry can)
FD Cheddar Cheese (1 pantry can)

EGGS IN A JAR

1/4 cup Dried Egg Powder
1 T. FD Chopped Onions
2 T. FD Green Bell Peppers
2 T. FD Mushrooms
2 T. FD Sausage Crumbles (optional)
1 T. FD Cheddar Cheese (optional)

When ready to serve, add 1/2 cup water to your jar and shake well. Spray a large coffee mug with pam spray and pour egg mixture in. Microwave for 30 seconds and stir. Microwave for 1 more minute. Eat! You can also cook in a regular frying pan.

http://mealsinajar.net

Ingredients per Jar:

Makes 1 serving per half-pint jar

1/4 cup Dried Egg Powder
1 T. FD Chopped Onions
2 T. FD Green Bell Peppers
2 T. FD Mushrooms
2 T. FD Sausage Crumbles (optional)
1 T. FD Cheddar Cheese (optional)

Directions:

To make jar: Add ingredients to jar in order listed for a prettier jar, add ingredients in reverse order if you want to do heaping servings. Add an oxygen absorber or seal with a Foodsaver jar lid attachment.

To prepare: When ready to serve, add 1/2 cup water to your jar and shake well. Spray a large coffee mug with pam spray and pour egg mixture in. Microwave for 30 seconds and stir. Microwave for 1 more minute. Eat! You can also cook in a regular frying pan.

Fruity Blender Wheat Pancakes

Fruity Blender Wheat Pancakes

Bulk Batch Shopping List

Makes 11-12 quart-sized jars

Instant Milk Powder (1 #10 can)

Dried Egg Powder (1 pantry can)

FD Bananas (1 #10 can)

FD Apples (2 #10 cans)

Wheat Kernels (12 cups)

Salt

Baking Powder

Meals-in-a-Jar
Made Easy

BLENDER PANCAKES

1 tsp. Baking Powder
1 pinch of Salt
1/4 c. Instant Milk Powder
6 T. Dried Egg Powder
1 c. Wheat Kernels
1 c. FD Bananas
1 1/3 c. FD Apples

Add two cups of water into a blender. Pour contents of jar on top. Blend for 4-5 minutes or run the "batter" setting 3-4 times. Make sure the batter is smooth or you will have gritty pancakes. Cook like regular pancakes and serve with your favorite toppings. I like to make a fruit compote using a mix of freeze-dried berries.

http://mealsinajar.net

Ingredients per Jar:

Makes 6-8 pancakes per quart jar

1 tsp. Baking Powder
1 pinch of Salt
1/4 c. Instant Milk Powder
6 T. Dried Egg Powder
1 c. Wheat Kernels (or 1 1/4 c. Flour)
1 c. FD Bananas
1 1/3 c. FD Apples (broken into smaller chunks)

Directions:

To make jar: Add ingredients to jar in order listed for a prettier jar, add ingredients in reverse order if you want to do heaping servings. Add an oxygen absorber or seal with a Foodsaver jar lid attachment.

To prepare: Add two cups of water into a blender. Pour contents of jar on top. Blend for 4-5 minutes or run the "batter" setting 3-4 times. Make sure the batter is smooth or you will have gritty pancakes. Cook like regular pancakes and serve with your favorite toppings. I like to make a fruit compote using a mix of freeze-dried berries.

Tip: To mix things up you can also cook these up as waffles and they are just as delicious!

Oatmeal in a Jar

Oatmeal in a Jar

Bulk Batch Shopping List

Makes 20-24 half-pint-sized jars

Honey Crystals (1 pantry can)

Instant Milk Powder (1 pantry can)

FD Fruit of Choice (1 #10 can)

Quick Oats (8 cups)

Cinnamon

Vanilla Powder (optional)

Ingredients per Jar:

Makes 1 serving per half-pint jar

1/4 tsp. Cinnamon
1 T. Honey Crystals or Sugar*
1 T. Instant Milk Powder
1/3 c. Quick Oats
1/2 c. of Freeze-Dried Fruit of Choice
1/2 tsp. of Vanilla Powder (optional)

**Feel free to substitute for any sweetener of choice*

Directions:

To make jar: Add ingredients to jar in order listed for a prettier jar, add ingredients in reverse order if you want to do heaping servings. Add an oxygen absorber or seal with a Foodsaver jar lid attachment.

To prepare: Add 1/2 cup of hot water to the jar, shake up and enjoy in 3-5 minutes.

OATMEAL IN A JAR

1/3 to 1/2 c. Quick Oats
1 T. Honey Crystals or Sugar
1 T. Instant Milk Powder
1/2 c. of FD Fruit of Choice
1/4 tsp. Cinnamon
1/2 tsp. of Vanilla Powder (optional)

Add 1/2 cup of hot water to the jar, shake up and enjoy in 3-5 minutes.

http://mealsinajar.net

Southwest Breakfast Casserole

Southwest Breakfast Casserole

Bulk Batch Shopping List

Makes 15-16 pint-sized jars

Dried Egg Powder (1 #10 can)

Instant Milk Powder (1 pantry can)

FD Chopped Onions (1 pantry can)

FD Green Chili Peppers (1 pantry can)

TFD Sausage (1 pantry can)

FD Cheddar Cheese (1 pantry can)

FD Red Bell Peppers (1 pantry can)

FD Diced Tomatoes (1 pantry can)

Spices

Meals-in-a-Jar Made Easy

BREAKFAST CASSEROLE

1/2 c. Dried Egg Powder
1 T. Instant Milk Powder
1/2 tsp. Cumin
1/2 tsp. Chili Powder
1/2 tsp. Salt
1/4 tsp. Pepper
1 T. FD Chopped Onions
2 T. FD Green Chili Peppers
1/4 c. FD Sausage
1/4 c. FD Cheddar Cheese
1/4 c. FD Red Bell Peppers
1/4 c. FD Diced Tomatoes

Mix contents of jar with 1 1/2 cups of water. Spray pam spray in a bread loaf pan or small round baking dish. Pour egg mixture into pan. Cover with tinfoil. Bake at 375 degrees for 45 minutes or until cooked through.

http://mealsinajar.net

Ingredients per Jar:

Makes 2-3 servings per pint jar

1/2 c. Dried Egg Powder
1 T. Instant Milk Powder
1/2 tsp. Cumin
1/2 tsp. Chili Powder
1/2 tsp. Salt
1/4 tsp. Pepper
1 T. FD Chopped Onions
2 T. FD Green Chili Peppers
1/4 c. FD Sausage
1/4 c. FD Cheddar Cheese
1/4 c. FD Red Bell Peppers
1/4 c. FD Diced Tomatoes

Directions:

To make jar: Add ingredients to jar in order listed for a prettier jar, add ingredients in reverse order if you want to do heaping servings. Add an oxygen absorber or seal with a Foodsaver jar lid attachment.

To prepare: Mix contents of jar with 1 1/2 cups of water. Spray pam spray in a bread loaf pan or small round baking dish. Pour egg mixture into pan. Cover with tinfoil. Bake at 375 degrees for 45 minutes or until cooked through.

Keep your friends close and your snacks closer!

SIDES / SNACKS

Banana Nut Bread

Banana Nut Bread

Bulk Batch Shopping List

Makes 11-12 jars sets

Dried Egg Powder(1 pantry can)

Dehydrated Applesauce (1 #10 can)

FD Bananas (1 #10 can + 1 pantry can)

FD Pineapple (1 #10 can)

Flour* (18 cups)

Sugar (12 cups)

Salt

Ground Cinnamon

Baking Soda

Vanilla Powder

**This recipe works well with gluten-free flour, you will need two #10 cans*

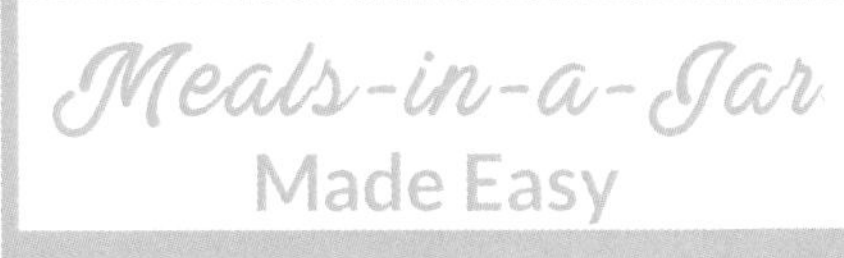

BANANA NUT BREAD

Jar 1 (quart):
1 1/2 c. White Flour
1/2 tsp. Baking Soda
1 c. White Sugar
1/4 tsp. Salt
1/2 tsp. Ground Cinnamon
3 T. Dried Egg Powder
1 tsp. Vanilla Powder
1/2 c. Dehydrated Applesauce
1/2 c. Chopped Pecans
Jar 2 (pint):
1 c. FD Bananas
1/2 c. FD Pineapple
Pour 1/2 cup of water into Jar 2. Wait 10 minutes, then mash up with a fork. Remove baggie from Jar 1. Combine remaining ingredients with 3/4 cups of water. Stir in pecans. Add mashed fruit and stir well. Bake at 350 for 60-70 minutes. Cool in pan for 10 minutes. Then cool on a wire rack.

http://mealsinajar.net

Ingredients per Jar:

Makes 1 loaf of bread per jar set

Jar 1 (quart):
1 1/2 c. White Flour
1/2 tsp. Baking Soda
1 c. White Sugar
1/4 tsp. Salt
1/2 tsp. Ground Cinnamon
3 T. Dried Egg Powder
1 tsp. Vanilla Powder
1/2 c. Dehydrated Applesauce
1/2 c. Chopped Pecans (in baggie)

Jar 2 (pint):
1 c. FD Bananas* (in chunks)
1/2 c. FD Pineapple* (crushed)

**Crush up the fruits first before measuring, you will need slightly more than these amounts to start with*

Directions:

To make jar: Add ingredients to each jar in order listed above. Place pecans in a separate ziplock bag and place at the top of the quart-sized jar. (Smash bananas and pineapples into smaller pieces BEFORE measuring) Add an oxygen absorber to each jar or seal with a Foodsaver jar lid attachment.

To prepare: Pour 1/2 cup of water into Jar 2. Wait 10 minutes, then mash up with a fork. Remove baggie from Jar 1. Combine remaining ingredients with 3/4 cups of water. Stir in pecans. Add mashed fruit and stir well. Bake at 350 for 60-70 minutes. Cool in pan for 10 minutes. Then cool on a wire rack.

Cranberry/Mango Muffins

Cranberry/Mango Muffins

Bulk Batch Shopping List

Makes 11-12 jars sets

Dried Egg Powder(1 pantry can)

Instant Milk Powder (1 pantry can)

FD Applesauce (1 pantry can)

FD Cranberries (1 #10 can)

FD Mango Chunks (1 #10 can)

White Flour (24 cups)

White Sugar (9 cups)

Salt

Baking Powder

Ingredients per Jar:

Makes 12 muffins per jar set

Jar 1 (quart):
2 c. White Flour
2 tsp. Baking Powder
3/4 c. White Sugar
1/8 tsp. Salt
2 T. Dried Egg Powder
3 T. Instant Milk Powder
2 T. FD Applesauce

Jar 2 (pint):
1 c. FD Cranberries
1 c. FD Mango Chunks

Directions:

To make jar: Add ingredients to each jar in the order listed above. Add an oxygen absorber to both jars or seal with a Foodsaver jar lid attachment.

To prepare: Combine jar contents with 1 1/2 cups of water and stir gently with a large spoon. Spoon into muffin tins (should make 12 muffins). Bake for 20-25 minutes at 400 degrees.

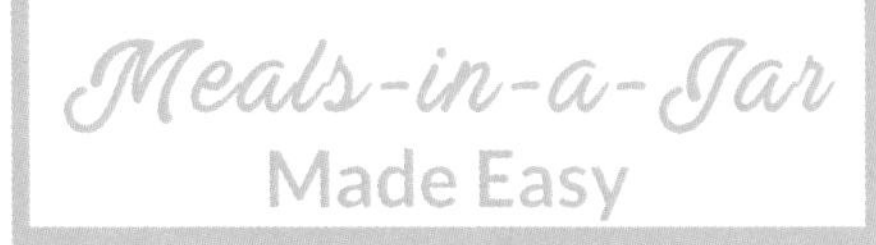

CRAN/MANGO MUFFINS

Jar 1 (quart):
2 c. White Flour
2 tsp. Baking Powder
3/4 c. White Sugar
1/8 tsp. Salt
2 T. Dried Egg Powder
3 T. Instant Milk Powder
2 T. FD Applesauce

Jar 2 (pint):
1 c. FD Cranberries
1 c. FD Mango Chunks

Combine jar contents with 1 1/2 cups of water and stir gently with a large spoon. Spoon into muffin tins (should make 12 muffins). Bake for 20-25 minutes at 400 degrees.

http://mealsinajar.net

Mountain Man Trail Mix

Mountain Man Trail Mix

Bulk Batch Shopping List

Makes 20-22 pint-sized jars

FD Shredded Cheddar Cheese (1 #10 can)

FD Sausage Crumbles (1 #10 can)

FD Sweet Corn (1 #10 can)

FD Green Peas (1 #10 can)

Seasoned Salt

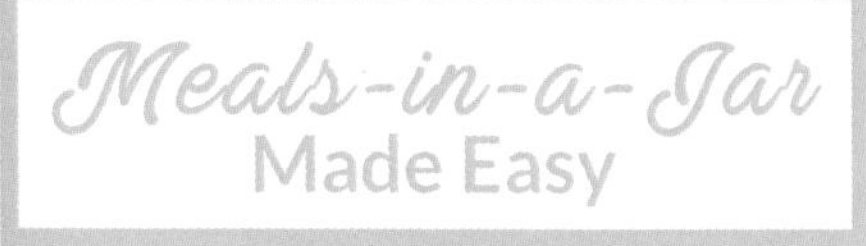

MOUNTAIN MAN MIX

1 tsp. Seasoned Salt
1/3 c. FD Shredded Cheddar Cheese
1/3 c. FD Sausage Crumbles
1/2 c. FD Sweet Corn
1/2 c. FD Green Peas

Pour contents into a bowl and stir up. Eat dry and enjoy!

http://mealsinajar.net

Ingredients per Jar:

Makes 4 servings per pint jar

1 tsp. Seasoned Salt
1/3 c. FD Shredded Cheddar Cheese
1/3 c. FD Sausage Crumbles
1/2 c. FD Sweet Corn
1/2 c. FD Green Peas

Directions:

To make jar: Mix all ingredients in a bowl and then pour entire contents into a pint-sized jar. Add an oxygen absorber or seal with a Foodsaver jar lid attachment.

To prepare: Pour contents into a bowl and stir up. Eat dry and enjoy!

Tip: You can also store this mix in ziplock bags, foodsaver bags, or mylar bags to make it lightweight and easier to grab and go for camping without worrying about breaking jars.

Muffin Mix

Muffin Mix

Bulk Batch Shopping List

Makes 7-8 quart-sized jars

Instant Milk Powder (1 pantry can)

Butter Powder (1 pantry cans)

Dried Egg Powder (1 pantry can)

FD Fruit of Choice (1 #10 can)

White Flour (16 cups)

White Sugar (4 cups)

Baking Powder

Salt

Ingredients per Jar:

Makes 12 large or 18 small muffins per quart jar

2 c. White Flour
1/2 c. White Sugar
2 tsp. Baking Powder
1 tsp. Salt
3 T. Instant Milk Powder
1/2 c. Butter Powder
2 T. Dried Egg Powder
1 c. FD Fruit of Choice (separate bag)

Directions:

To make jar: Add 1st 7 ingredients to jar in order listed. Store with 1 cup of fruit in a ziplock baggie taped to the jar or in a half-pint jar. Add an oxygen absorber or seal with a Foodsaver jar lid attachment.

To prepare: Combine contents of jar with 2 cups of water and mix with a hand mixer. Gently stir in freeze-dried fruit (can break into smaller pieces if desired). Pour into muffin tins and bake at 350 for 25-30 minutes.

MUFFIN MIX

2 c. White Flour
1/2 c. White Sugar
2 tsp. Baking Powder
1 tsp. Salt
3 T. Instant Milk Powder
1/2 c. Butter Powder
2 T. Dried Egg Powder
1 c. FD Fruit of Choice (separate bag)

Combine contents of jar with 2 cups of water and mix with a hand mixer. Gently stir in freeze-dried fruit (can break into smaller pieces if desired). Pour into muffin tins and bake at 350 for 25-30 minutes.

http://mealsinajar.net

Smoothie Mix

Smoothie Mix

Bulk Batch Shopping List

Makes 11-12 quart-sized jars

Instant Milk Powder (1 pantry can)

FD Spinach (1 pantry can)

FD Zucchini (2 pantry cans)

FD Pineapples (1 #10 can)

FD Apples (1 #10 can)

FD Mangos (2 pantry cans)

FD Bananas (2 pantry cans)

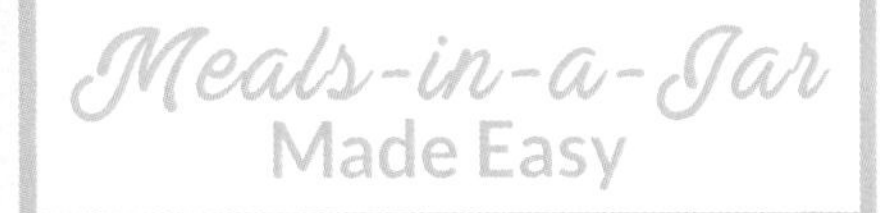

SMOOTHIE MIX

1/3 c. Instant Milk Powder
1/4 c. FD Spinach
1/2 c. FD Zucchini
3/4 c. FD Pineapples
3/4 c. FD Apples
1/2 c. FD Mango
1/2 c. FD Bananas

Add 2 cups of water and 1 cup of ice to a blender. Pour in the contents of the jar and blend well. Serve in a quart-sized mason jar.

http://mealsinajar.net

Ingredients per Jar:

Makes 1 smoothie per quart jar

1/3 c. Instant Milk Powder
1/4 c. FD Spinach
1/2 c. FD Zucchini
3/4 c. FD Pineapples
3/4 c. FD Apples
1/2 c. FD Mango
1/2 c. FD Bananas

Directions:

To make jar: Add ingredients to jar in order listed for a prettier jar, add ingredients in reverse order if you want to do heaping servings. Add an oxygen absorber or seal with a Foodsaver jar lid attachment.

To prepare: Add 2 cups of water and 1 cup of ice to a blender. Pour in the contents of the jar and blend well. Serve in a quart-sized mason jar.

Dinner is where
the magic happens
in the kitchen.

MAIN COURSES: PORK

Homemade Pizza

Homemade Pizza

Bulk Batch Shopping List

Makes 11-12 quart-sized jars

Thrive Tomato Sauce Mix (1 pantry can)
FD Mozzarella Cheese (1 #10 can)
FD Sausage (1 pantry can)
FD Chopped Onions (1 pantry can)
FD Mushrooms (1 pantry can)
White Flour (18 cups)
Instant Yeast
Salt

**This recipe works well with gluten-free flour, you will need two #10 cans*

Meals-in-a-Jar Made Easy

HOMEMADE PIZZA

1 1/2 c. White Flour
1/2 T. Instant Yeast
1/2 tsp. Salt
3 T. Thrive Tomato Sauce Mix
1/2 c. FD Mozzarella Cheese
1/3 c. FD Sausage
1/4 c. FD Chopped Onions
1/3 c. FD Mushrooms
Option: Other Veggies or Pineapple

Mix bread baggie with 1/2 c. water and 1 T. oil. Knead 5 mins. Make a 10 inch pizza crust. Let raise 1/2 hour. Bake at 350 for 10 minutes. In separate bowls rehydrate cheese and veggies. Drain excess water. Mix tomato powder with 1/2 c. boiling water. Spread onto cooked crust. Add refreshed cheese, veggies, and any optional toppings. Cook 10 more minutes.

http://mealsinajar.net

Ingredients per Jar:

Makes 1 10-inch pizza per quart jar

1 1/2 c. White Flour
1/2 T. Instant Yeast
1/2 tsp. Salt
3 T. Thrive Tomato Sauce Mix
1/2 c. FD Mozzarella Cheese
1/3 c. FD Sausage
1/4 c. FD Chopped Onions
1/3 c. FD Mushrooms
Other Veggies (or pineapple!) (optional)

Directions:

To make jar: Put 1st 3 ingredients into a ziplock baggie. Put tomato sauce in a separate baggie. Put mozzarella cheese in a separate baggie. Put the toppings into one final baggie. Put all baggies into jar. Add an oxygen absorber or seal with a Foodsaver jar lid attachment.

To prepare: Mix bread baggie with 1/2 c. water and 1 T. oil. Knead 5 mins. Make a 10 inch pizza crust. Let raise 1/2 hour. Bake at 350 for 10 minutes. In separate bowls rehydrate cheese and veggies. Drain excess water. Mix tomato powder with 1/2 c. boiling water. Spread onto cooked crust. Add refreshed cheese, veggies, and any optional toppings. Cook 10 more minutes.

One Pot Jambalaya

One-Pot Jambalaya

Bulk Batch Shopping List

Makes 11-12 quart-sized jars

FD Green Onions (1 pantry can)

FD Green Chili Peppers (1 pantry can)

FD Onion Slices (1 pantry can)

FD Tomato Dices (2 pantry cans)

FD Bell Peppers (2 pantry cans)

FD Sausage Crumbles (2 pantry cans)

FD Chicken Dices (1 #10 can)

Instant Rice (9 cups)

Minced Garlic

Ground Pepper

Salt

Cajun Seasoning

JAMBALAYA

1/4 tsp. Ground Pepper
1/2 tsp. Salt
1/2 T. Cajun Seasoning
1 tsp. Minced Garlic
1 T. FD Green Onions
2 T. FD Green Chili Peppers
1/3 c. FD Onion Slices
1/2 c. FD Tomato Dices
2/3 c. FD Bell Peppers (red or green)
1/2 c. FD Sausage Crumbles
3/4 c. FD Grilled Chicken Dices
3/4 c. Instant Rice

Mix contents of jar with 2 3/4 cups of water in a large saucepan. Bring to a boil then reduce heat and simmer for 20 minutes or until all water has been absorbed.

http://mealsinajar.net

Ingredients per Jar:

Makes 3-4 servings per quart jar

1/4 tsp. Ground Pepper
1/2 tsp. Salt
1/2 T. Cajun Seasoning
1 tsp. Minced Garlic
1 T. FD Green Onions
2 T. FD Green Chili Peppers
1/3 c. FD Onion Slices
1/2 c. FD Tomato Dices
2/3 c. FD Bell Peppers (red and/or green)
1/2 c. FD Sausage Crumbles
3/4 c. FD Grilled Chicken Dices
3/4 c. Instant Rice

Directions:

To make jar: Add ingredients to jar in order listed for a prettier jar, add ingredients in reverse order if you want to do heaping servings. Add an oxygen absorber or seal with a Foodsaver jar lid attachment.

To prepare: Mix contents of jar with 2 3/4 cups of water in a large saucepan. Bring to a boil then reduce heat and simmer for 20 minutes or until all water has been absorbed.

Pork Rice Skillet

Pork Rice Skillet

Bulk Batch Shopping List

Makes 14-15 quart-sized jars

FD Pulled Pork (1 #10 can)
FD Diced Tomatoes (2 pantry cans)
FD Green Bell Peppers (2 pantry cans)
Instant Black Beans (2 pantry cans)
FD Sweet Corn (2 pantry cans)
FD Chopped Onions (1 pantry can)
Instant Rice (7.5 cups)
Minced Garlic

Ingredients per Jar:

Makes 4-5 servings per quart jar

1 tsp. Minced Garlic
1/4 c. FD Chopped Onions
1/2 c. Instant Rice
1/2 c. FD Sweet Corn
1/2 c. Instant Black Beans
1/2 c. FD Green Bell Peppers
1/2 c. FD Diced Tomatoes
2/3 c. FD Pulled Pork

2 T. Vegetable Oil
3 c. Water
2/3 c. BBQ Sauce

Directions:

To make jar: Add 1st 8 ingredients into the jar in the order listed. Shake the jar a little bit at each layer to sprinkle the products down into the jar. It won't look like pretty layers but it will fit more food in it!

To prepare: Heat vegetable oil in a medium skillet. Add contents of jar and sauté for 1-2 minutes. Add water and bring to a boil. Simmer for 10 minutes or until rice and beans are softened. Stir in BBQ sauce and heat until warm. ENJOY!

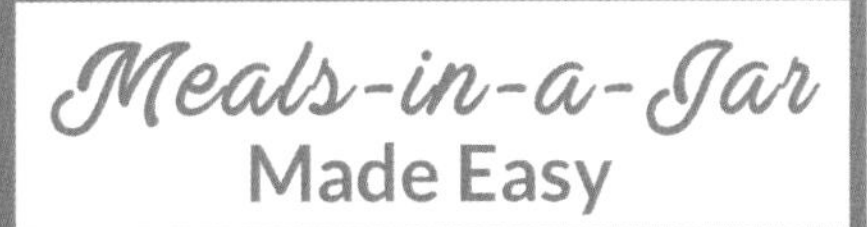

PORK RICE SKILLET

1 tsp. Minced Garlic
1/4 c. FD Chopped Onions
1/2 c. Instant Rice
1/2 c. FD Sweet Corn
1/2 c. Instant Black Beans
1/2 c. FD Green Bell Peppers
1/2 c. FD Diced Tomatoes
2/3 c. FD Pulled Pork

2 T. Vegetable Oil
3 c. Water
2/3 c. BBQ Sauce

Put 2 T. vegetable oil into a medium sized skillet. Add entire contents of jar and saute for 1-2 minutes. Add 3 c. water and simmer for 8-10 minutes or until water is absorbed and rice and beans are softened. Stir in BBQ sauce and heat until warm.

http://mealsinajar.net

Sausage Lasagna

Sausage Lasagna

Bulk Batch Shopping List

Makes 11-12 quart-sized jars

Thrive Tomato Sauce Mix (2 pantry cans)

FD Mozzarella Cheese (#10 can)

FD Sausage Crumbles (#10 can)

FD Green Bell Peppers (#10 can)

Farfalle (Bowtie) Pasta (30 cups)

Ingredients per Jar:

Makes 4-5 servings per quart jar

1/2 c. Thrive Tomato Sauce Mix
1/2 c. FD Shredded Mozzarella Cheese
3/4 c. FD Sausage Crumbles
1/2 c. FD Green Bell Peppers
2 1/2 c. Farfalle (Bowtie) Pasta

Directions:

To make jar: Add ingredients to jar in order listed for a prettier jar, add ingredients in reverse order if you want to do heaping servings. Add an oxygen absorber or seal with a Foodsaver jar lid attachment.

To prepare: Pour contents of jar into a large frying pan. Add 3 1/4 cups of water. Bring to a boil. Turn heat to low and let simmer for 15 minutes stirring frequently. Let stand for 5 minutes to thicken. Enjoy!

Meals-in-a-Jar
Made Easy

SAUSAGE LASAGNA

1/2 c. Thrive Tomato Sauce Mix
1/2 c. FD Shredded Mozzarella
3/4 c. FD Sausage Crumbles
1/2 c. FD Green Bell Peppers
2 1/2 c. Farfalle (Bowtie) Pasta

Pour contents of jar into a large frying pan. Add 3 1/4 cups of water. Bring to a boil. Turn heat to low and let simmer for 15 minutes stirring frequently. Let stand for 5 minutes to thicken. Enjoy!

http://mealsinajar.net

Sweet 'n' Sour Pork

Sweet 'n' Sour Pork

Bulk Batch Shopping List

Makes 12-13 quart-sized jars

FD Green Onions (1 pantry can)
FD Onion Slices (2 pantry cans)
FD Red Pepper Slices (1 #10 can)
FD Pineapples (1 #10 can)
FD Pulled Pork (2 #10 cans)
Sweet and Sour Sauce Mix (13 packets)
Minced Garlic

Ingredients per Jar:

Makes 4-5 servings per quart jar

1 pkg. Sweet and Sour Sauce Mix
1 tsp. Minced Garlic
1/4 c. FD Green Onions
1/2 c. FD Onion Slices
3/4 c. FD Red Peppers
3/4 c. FD Pineapples
1 1/2 c. FD Pulled Pork

2 T. Soy Sauce
2 1/2 c. Water
2-3 c. Instant Rice

Directions:

To make jar: Add 1st 7 ingredients to jar in order listed for a prettier jar, add ingredients in reverse order if you want to do heaping servings. Measure out 2-3 cups of instant rice and put in a separate baggie beside the jar.

To prepare: In a medium saucepan combine water, soy sauce and contents of jar and bring to a boil. Let simmer for 12-15 minutes or until fully refreshed.

Meals-in-a-Jar
Made Easy

SWEET 'N' SOUR PORK

1 pkg. Sweet and Sour Sauce Mix
1 tsp. Minced Garlic
1/4 c. FD Green Onions
1/2 c. FD Onion Slices
3/4 c. FD Red Peppers
3/4 c. FD Pineapples
1 1/2 c. FD Pulled Pork

2 T. Soy Sauce
2 1/2 cups Water
2-3 cups Instant Rice

In a medium saucepan combine water, soy sauce and contents of jar and bring to a boil. Let simmer for 12-15 minutes or until fully refreshed.

http://mealsinajar.net

Zuppa Tuscana

Zuppa Tuscana

Bulk Batch Shopping List

Makes 13-14 quart-sized jars

Sour Cream Powder (1 pantry can)
Thrive Velouté Gravy (1 pantry can)
Chicken Bouillon (1 pantry can)
FD Chopped Onions (1 pantry can)
FD Spinach (1 #10 can)
FD Diced Potatoes (1 #10 can)
FD Sausage Crumbles (1 #10 can)
Dehydrated Mashed Potatoes (1 #10 can)
Seasoned Salt
Garlic Powder

Ingredients per Jar:

Makes 4-5 servings per quart jar

1/4 c. Sour Cream Powder
3 T. Thrive Velouté Gravy
1 T. Chicken Bouillon
3 T. FD Chopped Onions
1/2 tsp. Garlic Powder
1/2 tsp. Seasoned Salt
3/4 c. FD Spinach
3/4 c. FD Diced Potatoes
3/4 c. FD Sausage Crumbles
3/4 c. Dehydrated Mashed Potatoes

Directions:

To make jar: Add ingredients to jar in order listed for a prettier jar, add ingredients in reverse order if you want to do heaping servings. Add an oxygen absorber or seal with a Foodsaver jar lid attachment.

To prepare: Pour 5 cups of water into a large saucepan. Add contents of jar and stir thoroughly. Cook 10-12 minutes or until potatoes are soft.

Meals-in-a-Jar
Made Easy

ZUPPA TUSCANA

1/4 c. Sour Cream Powder
3 T. Thrive Velouté Gravy
1 T. Chicken Bouillon
3 T. FD Chopped Onions
1/2 tsp. Garlic Powder
1/2 tsp. Seasoned Salt
3/4 c. FD Spinach
3/4 c. FD Diced Potatoes
3/4 c. FD Sausage Crumbles
3/4 c. Dehydrated Mashed Potatoes

Pour 5 cups of water into a large saucepan. Add contents of jar and stir thoroughly. Cook 10-12 minutes or until potatoes are soft.

http://mealsinajar.net

The best memories
are made around
the dinner table.

MAIN COURSES: CHICKEN

Chicken Broccoli Bake

Chicken Broccoli Bake

Bulk Batch Shopping List

Makes 10-11 quart-sized jars

Thrive Velouté Gravy (1 pantry can)
FD Chopped Onions (1 pantry can)
FD Cheddar Cheese (1 pantry can)
FD Chopped Chicken (1 #10 can)
FD Broccoli (1 #10 can)
Instant White Rice (14 cups)
Seasoned Salt

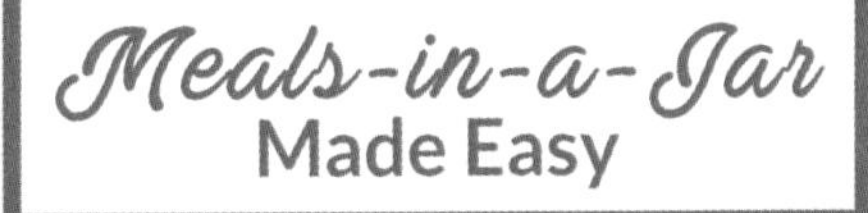

CHICKEN BAKE

1/3 cup Thrive Velouté Gravy
1 tsp. Seasoned Salt
2 T. FD Chopped Onions
1/3 cup FD Cheddar Cheese
1 1/4 cup Instant White Rice
1 cup FD Chopped Chicken
1 cup FD Broccoli

Combine ingredients with 3 1/4 cups of water in a 9×9 casserole dish. Bake at 350° for 30 minutes, stir halfway through.

http://mealsinajar.net

Ingredients per Jar:

Makes 4-5 servings per quart jar

1/3 c. Thrive Velouté Gravy
1 tsp. Seasoned Salt
2 T. FD Chopped Onions
1/3 c. FD Cheddar Cheese
1 1/4 c. Instant White Rice
1 c. FD Chopped Chicken
1 c. FD Broccoli (or corn or other veggie)

Directions:

To make jar: Add ingredients to jar in order listed for a prettier jar, add ingredients in reverse order if you want to do heaping servings. Add an oxygen absorber or seal with a Foodsaver jar lid attachment.

To prepare: Combine ingredients with 3 1/4 cups of water in a 9×9 casserole dish. Bake at 350° for 30 minutes, stir halfway through.

Chicken Chili

Chicken Chili

Bulk Batch Shopping List

Makes 10-11 quart-sized jars

Chicken Bouillon (1 pantry can)

Thrive Tomato Sauce Mix (1 pantry can)

FD Green Chili Peppers (1 pantry can)

FD Chopped Onions (1 pantry can)

Instant Black Beans (1 #10 can)

FD Sweet Corn (2 pantry cans)

FD Chopped Chicken (1 #10 can)

FD Tomato Dices (1 pantry can)

Instant White Rice (6 cups)

Chili Powder

Minced Garlic

Cumin

CHICKEN CHILI

1 tsp. Chili Powder
1 tsp. Minced Garlic
1 tsp. Cumin
2 T. Chicken Bouillon
3 T. Thrive Tomato Sauce Mix
2 T. FD Green Chili Peppers
3 T. FD Onions
1/2 c. Instant Rice
3/4 c. Instant Black Beans
1/2 c. FD Sweet Corn
3/4 c. FD Chopped Chicken
1/4 c. FD Tomatoes

Combine contents of jar with 7-8 cups of water and bring to a boil. Reduce heat and let simmer for 15 minutes.

http://mealsinajar.net

Ingredients per Jar:

Makes 4-5 servings per quart jar

1 tsp. Chili Powder
1 tsp. Minced Garlic
1 tsp. Cumin
2 T. Chicken Bouillon
3 T. Thrive Tomato Sauce Mix
2 T. FD Green Chili Peppers
3 T. FD Chopped Onions
1/2 c. Instant Rice
3/4 c. Instant Black Beans
1/2 c. FD Sweet Corn
3/4 c. FD Chopped Chicken
1/4 c. FD Tomatoes

Directions:

To make jar: Add ingredients to jar in order listed for a prettier jar, add ingredients in reverse order if you want to do heaping servings. Add an oxygen absorber or seal with a Foodsaver jar lid attachment.

To prepare: Combine contents of jar with 7-8 cups of water and bring to a boil. Reduce heat and let simmer for 15 minutes.

Chicken Fajitas

Chicken Fajitas

Bulk Batch Shopping List

Makes 10-11 quart-sized jars

FD Green Bell Peppers (1 #10 can)
FD Seasoned Chicken Slices (1 #10 can)
FD Onion Slices (1 #10 can)
FD Red Bell Peppers (1 #10 can)
FD Green Chili Peppers (1 pantry can)
Seasoned Salt
Cilantro
Ground Cumin
Chili Powder
Garlic Powder
Lime Powder (optional)

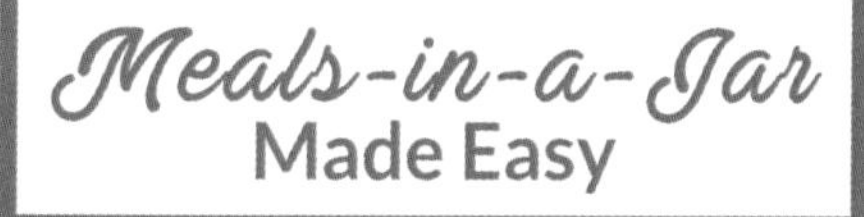

CHICKEN FAJITAS

3/4 c. FD Green Bell Peppers
1 c. FD Seasoned Chicken Slices
3/4 c. FD Onion Slices
3/4 c. FD Red Bell Peppers
1/4 c. FD Green Chili Peppers
1/2 tsp. Seasoned Salt
1/2 tsp. Dehydrated Cilantro
1/2 tsp. Ground Cumin
1/2 tsp. Chili Powder
1/4 tsp. Garlic Powder
1/4 tsp. Lime Powder (optional)

Add contents of jar to 2 cups of warm water and let sit for 8 minutes. Drain off excess water. Heat 1 tbsp. of oil in skillet. Add chicken mixture. Stir until golden browned. Serve on flour tortillas and top with cheese, sour cream, salsa or guacamole.

http://mealsinajar.net

Ingredients per Jar:

Makes 3-4 servings per quart jar

1/2 tsp. Seasoned Salt
1/2 tsp. Cilantro
1/2 tsp. Ground Cumin
1/2 tsp. Chili Powder
1/4 tsp. Garlic Powder
1/4 tsp. Lime Powder (optional)
1/4 c. FD Green Chili Peppers
3/4 c. FD Onion Slices
3/4 c. FD Green Bell Peppers
3/4 c. FD Red Bell Peppers
1 c. FD Seasoned Chicken Slices

Directions:

To make jar: Add ingredients to jar in order listed for a prettier jar, add ingredients in reverse order if you want to do heaping servings. Add an oxygen absorber or seal with a Foodsaver jar lid attachment.

To prepare: Add contents of jar to 2 cups of warm water and let sit for 8 minutes. Drain off excess water. Add 1 tbsp. of oil to skillet and heat until hot. Add chicken mixture and stir until lightly browned. Serve on flour tortillas and top with cheese, sour cream, salsa or guacamole.

Chicken Fried Rice

Chicken Fried Rice

Bulk Batch Shopping List

Makes 10-11 quart-sized jars

FD Chopped Onions (1 pantry can)
FD Spinach (1 pantry can)
FD Sweet Corn (1 pantry can)
FD Peas (1 pantry can)
FD Red Bell Peppers (1 pantry can)
FD Zucchini (1 pantry can)
FD Chopped Chicken (1 #10 can)
Dried Egg Powder (1 pantry can)
Instant Rice (22 cups)

CHICKEN FRIED RICE

1/4 c. FD Chopped Onions
1/3 c. FD Spinach
1/3 c. FD Sweet Corn
1/3 c. FD Peas
1/3 c. FD Red Bell Peppers
1/3 c. FD Zucchini
1 c. FD Chopped Chicken
1/4 c. Dried Egg Powder

Remove baggie containing egg mix from jar. Combine egg mix with 6 T. water. Scramble eggs and break into small chunks. Combine contents of jar and 6 cups of water in a pan. Bring to a boil, then add rice. Cook on low 8-10 minutes. Let stand for 5-7 minutes. Stir in 3T. soy sauce, adding more to taste if desired.

http://mealsinajar.net

Ingredients per Jar:

Makes 6-7 side dish servings per quart jar

1/4 c. FD Chopped Onions
1/3 c. FD Spinach
1/3 c. FD Sweet Corn
1/3 c. FD Peas
1/3 c. FD Red Bell Peppers
1/3 c. FD Zucchini
1 c. FD Chopped Chicken
1/4 c. Dried Egg Powder (separate bag)

For Serving:

2 c. Instant Rice
3 T. Soy Sauce

Directions:

To make jar: Add 1st 7 ingredients to jar in order listed for a prettier jar, add ingredients in reverse order if you want to do heaping servings. Include scrambled egg mix in a separate baggie inside the jar. Store with 2 cups of rice in a pint size jar beside the jar. Add an oxygen absorber or seal with a Foodsaver jar lid attachment.

To prepare: Remove baggie containing egg mix from jar. Combine egg mix with 6 T. water. Scramble eggs and break into small chunks. Combine contents of jar with 6 cups of water in large saucepan. Bring to a boil, and add rice. Cook on low 8-10 minutes. Let stand for 5-7 minutes. Stir in 3T. soy sauce or more to taste.

Chicken Noodle Soup

Chicken Noodle Soup

Bulk Batch Shopping List

Makes 10-11 quart-sized jars

Chicken Bouillon (1 pantry can)

FD Chopped Onions (1 pantry can)

Dehydrated Carrot Dices (1 pantry can)

FD Celery (2 pantry cans)

FD Chopped Chicken (1 #10 can)

Egg Noodle Pasta (22 cups)

Seasoned Salt

Garlic Powder

Salt

CHICKEN NOODLE SOUP

2 T. Chicken Bouillon
2 tsp. Seasoned Salt
2 tsp. Garlic Salt
1 tsp. salt (or more to taste)
1/4 c. FD Chopped Onions
1/4 c. Dehydrated Carrot Dices
1/2 c. FD Celery
1 c. FD Chopped Chicken
2 c. Egg Noodle Pasta

Bring 8 cups of water to a boil in a large saucepan. Add jar ingredients and simmer for 30 minutes or until carrots are softened.

http://mealsinajar.net

Ingredients per Jar:

Makes 4-5 servings per quart jar

2 T. Chicken Bouillon
2 tsp. Seasoned Salt
2 tsp. Garlic Powder
1 tsp. Salt (or more to taste)
1/4 c. FD Chopped Onions
1/4 c. Dehydrated Carrot Dices
1/2 c. FD Celery
1 c. FD Chopped Chicken
2 c. Egg Noodle Pasta (or any favorite pasta)

Directions:

To make jar: Add ingredients to jar in order listed for a prettier jar, add ingredients in reverse order if you want to do heaping servings. Add an oxygen absorber or seal with a Foodsaver jar lid attachment.

To prepare: Bring 8 cups of water to a boil in a large saucepan. Add jar ingredients and simmer for 30 minutes or until carrots are softened.

Chicken Pot Pie

Chicken Pot Pie

Bulk Batch Shopping List

Makes 13-14 quart-sized jars

Thrive Velouté Gravy Mix (1 pantry can)
FD Chopped Onions (1 pantry can)
FD Celery (1 pantry can)
FD Green Peas (1 pantry can)
FD Sweet Corn (2 pantry cans)
FD Diced Potatoes (1 #10 can)
FD Chopped Chicken (1 #10 can)
Minced Garlic
Seasoned Salt

CHICKEN POT PIE

1 tsp. Minced Garlic
1 tsp. Seasoned Salt
1/4 c.. Thrive Velouté Gravy Mix
1/4 c. FD Chopped Onions
1/3 c. FD Celery
1/3 c. FD Green Peas
2/3 c. FD Sweet Corn
1 c. FD Diced Potatoes
1 c. FD Chopped Chicken

Pour 3 1/2 cups of water into a large saucepan. Add contents of jar and stir thoroughly. Cook 10-12 minutes or until potatoes are soft. Pour mixture into 1 pie crust set into a pie pan. Cover with remaining pie crust. Make small slices in the crust for venting. Cook at 350 for 20 minutes or until crust is golden brown.

http://mealsinajar.net

Ingredients per Jar:

Makes 1 pie per quart jar

1 tsp. Minced Garlic
1 tsp. Seasoned Salt
1/4 c.. Thrive Velouté Gravy Mix
1/4 c. FD Chopped Onions
1/3 c. FD Celery
1/3 c. FD Green Peas
2/3 c. FD Sweet Corn
1 c. FD Diced Potatoes
1 c. FD Chopped Chicken

2-pack Prepared Pie Crusts (for serving)

Directions:

To make jar: Add ingredients to jar in order listed for a prettier jar, add ingredients in reverse order if you want to do heaping servings. Add an oxygen absorber or seal with a Foodsaver jar lid attachment.

To prepare: Pour 3 1/2 cups of water into a large saucepan. Add contents of jar and stir thoroughly. Cook 10-12 minutes or until potatoes are soft. Pour mixture into 1 pie crust set into a pie pan. Cover with remaining pie crust. Make small slices in the crust for venting. Cook at 350 for 20 minutes or until crust is golden brown.

Chicken Quesadillas

Chicken Quesadillas

Bulk Batch Shopping List

Makes 13-14 quart-sized jars

FD Green Chili Peppers (1 pantry can)
FD Cheddar Cheese (1 #10 can)
Dehydrated Refried Beans (1 #10 can)
FD Tomato Dices (2 pantry cans)
FD Onion Slices (1 pantry can)
FD Grilled Chicken (1 #10 can)

Ingredients per Jar:

Makes 4-6 half-size quesadillas per quart jar

2 T. FD Green Chili Peppers
1 c. FD Cheddar Cheese
1 c. Dehydrated Refried Beans
1/3 c. FD Onion Slices
1/2 c. FD Tomato Dices
1 c. FD Grilled Chicken

1 pkg. Flour Tortillas (for serving)

Directions:

To make jar: Add ingredients to jar in order listed for a prettier jar, add ingredients in reverse order if you want to do heaping servings. Add an oxygen absorber or seal with a Foodsaver jar lid attachment.

To prepare: Pour contents of jar into a 4 cup measuring cup. Add 2 cups of water and let stand for 15 minutes until chicken is refreshed all the way, stirring if necessary. Drain off any excess water. Scoop mixture into 10-inch soft tortillas and either fold in half or cover with an additional tortilla. Cook on a greased skillet for 3 minutes on each side or until golden brown. Let stand for 5 minutes after cooking to thicken up.

Meals-in-a-Jar Made Easy

CHICKEN QUESADILLA

2 T. FD Green Chili Peppers
1 c. FD Cheddar Cheese
1 c. Dehydrated Refried Beans
1/2 c. FD Tomato Dices
1/3 c. FD Onion Slices
1 c. FD Grilled Chicken

Pour contents of jar into a 4 cup measuring cup. Add 2 cups of water and let stand for 15 minutes until chicken is refreshed all the way, stirring if necessary. Drain off any excess water. Scoop mixture into 10-inch soft tortillas and either fold in half or cover with an additional tortilla. Cook on a greased skillet for 3 minutes on each side or until golden brown. Let stand for 5 minutes after cooking to thicken up.

http://mealsinajar.net

Chicken Taco Bake

Chicken Taco Bake

Bulk Batch Shopping List

Makes 10-11 quart-sized jars

FD Seasoned Chicken Slices (1 #10 can)

FD Red Bell Peppers (1 #10 can)

FD Green Chili Peppers (1 pantry can)

FD Chopped Onions (1 pantry can)

Tomato Powder (1 pantry can)

Instant White Rice (18 cups)

Taco Seasoning (11 packets)

Minced Garlic

Salt

CHICKEN TACO BAKE

3/4 c. FD Seasoned Chicken Slices
3/4 c. FD Red Bell Peppers
1/4 c. FD Green Chili Peppers
1 1/2 c. Instant White Rice
1/4 c. FD Chopped Onions
1 packet Taco Seasoning
1 tsp. Minced Garlic
1/4 c. Tomato Powder
1 1/2 tsp. Salt

Add contents of jar and 5 1/2 cups of water to your InstantPot or other electric pressure cooker. Use the rice setting or cook on low pressure for 12 minutes. After you release the pressure let stand for 5-10 minutes to thicken. If using a saucepan cook on low for 20 minutes and let stand for 10 minutes.

http://mealsinajar.net

Ingredients per Jar:

Makes 5-6 small servings per quart jar

3/4 c. FD Seasoned Chicken Slices
3/4 c. FD Red Bell Peppers
1/4 c. FD Green Chili Peppers
1 1/2 c. Instant White Rice
1/4 c. FD Chopped Onions
1 packet Taco Seasoning
1 tsp. Minced Garlic
1/4 c. Tomato Powder
1 1/2 tsp. Salt

Directions:

To make jar: Add ingredients to jar in order listed for a prettier jar, add ingredients in reverse order if you want to do heaping servings. Add an oxygen absorber or seal with a Foodsaver jar lid attachment.

To prepare: Add contents of jar and 5 1/2 cups of water to your InstantPot or other electric pressure cooker. Use the rice setting or cook on low pressure for 12 minutes. After you release the pressure let stand for 5-10 minutes to thicken. If using a saucepan cook on low for 20 minutes and let stand for 10 minutes. Serve in a soft taco shell, as a taco salad, or by itself as a casserole.

Chicken Tortilla Soup

Chicken Tortilla Soup

Bulk Batch Shopping List

Makes 10-11 quart-sized jars

Chicken Bouillon (1 pantry can)
Tomato Powder (1 pantry can)
FD Green Chili Peppers (1 pantry can)
FD Onion Slices (1 pantry can)
FD Sweet Corn (1 pantry can)
Instant Black Beans (1 #10 can)
FD Chicken Slices (1 #10 can)
FD Diced Tomatoes (1 #10 can)

Ingredients per Jar:

Makes 4-5 servings per quart jar

2 T. Chicken Bouillon
2 T. Tomato Powder
2 T. FD Green Chili Peppers
1/3 c. FD Onion Slices
1/3 c. FD Sweet Corn
3/4 c. Instant Black Beans
1 c. FD Chicken Slices
3/4 c. FD Diced Tomatoes

Directions:

To make jar: Add ingredients to jar in order listed for a prettier jar, add ingredients in reverse order if you want to do heaping servings. Add an oxygen absorber or seal with a Foodsaver jar lid attachment.

To prepare: Bring 5 cups of water to a boil in a large saucepan. Pour contents of jar into pot and stir. Let cook for 10-12 minutes or until beans are soft and soup is slightly thickened. Top with tortilla chips, sour cream, and cheese if desired!

CHICKEN TORTILLA SOUP

2 T. Chicken Bouillon
2 T. Tomato Powder
2 T. FD Green Chili Peppers
1/3 c. FD Onion Slices
1/3 c. FD Sweet Corn
3/4 c. Instant Black Beans
1 c. FD Chicken Slices
3/4 c. FD Diced Tomatoes

Bring 5 cups of water to a boil in a large saucepan. Pour contents of jar into pot and stir. Let cook for 10-12 minutes or until beans are soft and soup is slightly thickened. Top with tortilla chips, sour cream, and cheese if desired!

http://mealsinajar.net

Hawaiian Haystacks

Hawaiian Haystacks

Bulk Batch Shopping List

Makes 10-11 quart-sized jars

Thrive Velouté Sauce Mix (1 pantry can)
FD Chopped Onions (1 pantry can)
FD Chopped Chicken (1 #10 can)
FD Mozzarella Cheese (1 pantry can)
FD Pineapple (2 pantry cans)
FD Green Onions (1 pantry can)
Instant Rice (14 cups)
Chow Mein Noodles (3 cups)
Cocount Flakes
Minced Garlic
Salt

HAWAIIAN HAYSTACKS

1/4 c. Thrive Velouté Sauce Mix
2 T. FD Chopped Onions
3/4 c. FD Chopped Chicken
1 1/4 c. Instant Rice
1 tsp. Minced Garlic
1/2 tsp. Salt
1/4 c. FD Mozzarella Cheese
1/2 c. FD Pineapple
1 T. Coconut Flakes
2 tsp. FD Green Onions
1/4 c. Chow Mein Noodles

Boil 3 cups of water in large saucepan. Remove zip-lock bag from jar. Add first 6 ingredients to boiling water. Simmer for 7 minutes. Let sit 5 more minutes. Top with remaining 5 ingredients or any other yummy toppings (mandarin oranges, tomatoes, olives, etc.)

http://mealsinajar.net

Ingredients per Jar:

Makes 4-5 servings per quart jar

1/4 c. Thrive Velouté Sauce Mix
1 tsp. Minced Garlic
1/2 tsp. Salt
2 T. FD Chopped Onions
1 1/4 c. Instant Rice
3/4 c. FD Chopped Chicken
1/4 c. FD Mozzarella Cheese
1/2 c. FD Pineapple
1 T. Coconut Flakes
2 tsp. FD Green Onions
1/4 c. Chow Mein Noodles

Directions:

To make jar: Add 1st 6 ingredients into the jar in the order listed. Add remaining ingredients into a zip-lock bag and place into jar. Add an oxygen absorber or seal with a Foodsaver jar lid attachment.

To prepare: Boil 3 cups of water in large saucepan. Remove zip-lock bag from jar. Add first 6 ingredients to boiling water. Simmer for 7 minutes. Let sit 5 more minutes. Top with remaining 5 ingredients or any other yummy toppings (mandarin oranges, tomatoes, olives, etc.)

One-Pot Chicken Pasta

One-Pot Chicken Pasta

Bulk Batch Shopping List

Makes 11-12 quart-sized jars

Chicken Bouillon (1 pantry can)
Tomato Powder (1 pantry can)
FD Chopped Onion (1 pantry can)
FD Spinach (1 pantry can)
FD Peas (1 pantry can)
FD Grilled Chicken Dices (2 pantry cans)
FD Mozzarella Cheese (2 pantry cans)
FD Parmesan Cheese (1 pantry can)
FD Tomato Dices (1 pantry can)
Macaroni Noodles (13 cups)
Minced Garlic
Salt and Pepper

Meals-in-a-Jar
Made Easy

CHICKEN PASTA

3 tsp. Chicken Bouillon
1/2 tsp. Kosher Salt
1 tsp. Minced Garlic
1/4 tsp. Pepper
2 1/2 T. Tomato Powder
2 T. FD Chopped Onion
1/3 c. FD Spinach
1 1/4 c. Macaroni Noodles
1/4 c. FD Peas
2/3 c. FD Chopped Chicken
1/2 c. FD Mozzarella Cheese
2 T. FD Parmesan Cheese
1/3 c. FD Tomato Dices

Boil 3 1/2 cups of water in a large saucepan. Add contents of jar to the pot and stir. Reduce heat and simmer for 5 minutes. Remove from heat and let stand for 5-10 minutes or until water is all absorbed.

http://mealsinajar.net

Ingredients per Jar:

Makes 4-5 servings per quart jar

3 tsp. Chicken Bouillon
1/2 tsp. Kosher Salt
1 tsp. Minced Garlic
1/4 tsp. Pepper
2 1/2 T. Tomato Powder
2 T. FD Chopped Onion
1/3 c. FD Spinach
1 1/4 c. Macaroni Noodles (or favorite pasta)
1/4 c. FD Peas
2/3 c. FD Chopped Chicken
1/2 c. FD Mozzarella Cheese
2 T. FD Parmesan Cheese
1/3 c. FD Tomato Dices

Directions:

To make jar: Add ingredients to jar in order listed for a prettier jar, add ingredients in reverse order if you want to do heaping servings. Add an oxygen absorber or seal with a Foodsaver jar lid attachment.

To prepare: Bring 3 1/2 cups of water to a boil in a large saucepan. Add contents of jar and stir. Reduce heat to low and simmer for 5 minutes. Remove from heat, let stand for 5-10 minutes or until water is all absorbed.

Tortellini Soup

Tortellini Soup

Bulk Batch Shopping List

Makes 10-11 quart-sized jars

Chicken Bouillon (1 pantry can)

FD Chopped Onions (1 pantry can)

FD Celery (2 pantry cans)

FD Grilled Chicken (1 #10 can)

Dried 3-Cheese Tortellini Pasta (17 cups)

Celery Seed

Basil

Garlic Salt

Salt

Red Pepper Flakes (optional)

TORTELLINI SOUP

3 T. Chicken Bouillon
1/2 tsp. Celery Seed
1/2 tsp. Basil
1/2 tsp. Garlic Salt
1 tsp. Salt
1/4 c. FD Chopped Onions
1/2 c. FD Celery
1 c. FD Grilled Chicken
1 1/2 c. 3-Cheese Tortellini Pasta
Sprinkle of Red Pepper Flakes

Bring 9 cups of water to a boil. Add contents of jar and cook until tortellinis are soft.

http://mealsinajar.net

Ingredients per Jar:

Makes 4-5 servings per quart jar

3 T. Chicken Bouillon
1/2 tsp. Celery Seed
1/2 tsp. Basil
1/2 tsp. Garlic Salt
1 tsp. Salt
1/4 c. FD Chopped Onions
1/2 c. FD Celery
1 c. FD Grilled Chicken
1 1/2 c. Dried 3-Cheese Tortellini Pasta
Sprinkle of Red Pepper Flakes (optional)

Directions:

To make jar: Add ingredients to jar in order listed for a prettier jar, add ingredients in reverse order if you want to do heaping servings. Add an oxygen absorber or seal with a Foodsaver jar lid attachment.

To prepare: Bring 9 cups of water to a boil. Add contents of jar and cook until tortellinis are soft.

Food tastes better
when you eat it
with your family

MAIN COURSES: BEEF

Beef Rice-A-Roni

Beef Rice-A-Roni

Bulk Batch Shopping List

Makes 10-11 quart-sized jars

FD Ground Beef (1#10 can)
Beef Bouillon (1 pantry can)
FD Onions (1 pantry can)
White Rice (22 cups)
Fine Egg Noodle Pasta (11 cups)
Parsley
Onion Powder
Garlic Powder
Dried Thyme

BEEF RICE-A-RONI

2 T. Parsley
2 tsp. Onion Powder
½ tsp. Garlic Powder
¼ tsp. Dried Thyme
2 T. Beef Bouillon
2 c. White Rice
3 T. FD Onions
1 c. Fine Egg Noodle Pasta
1 c. FD Ground Beef
1/4 c. Butter (for serving)

Melt 1/4 c. butter in a large saucepan. Add contents of jar and stir around to let brown. Add 5 1/2 cups of water and bring to a boil. Reduce heat and let simmer for 15 minutes. Let stand for 5 minutes or until thickened.

http://mealsinajar.net

Ingredients per Jar:

Makes 6-8 side-dish servings per quart jar

2 T. Parsley
2 tsp. Onion Powder
½ tsp. Garlic Powder
¼ tsp. Dried Thyme
2 T. Beef Bouillon
2 c. White Rice
3 T. FD Onions
1 c. Fine Egg Noodle Pasta
1 c. FD Ground Beef

1/4 c. Butter (for serving)

Directions:

To make jar: Add ingredients to jar in order listed if you want to do heaping servings, or for a prettier jar, add ingredients in reverse order. Add an oxygen absorber or seal with a Foodsaver jar lid attachment.

To prepare: Melt 1/4 c. butter in a large saucepan. Add contents of jar and stir around to let brown. Add 5 1/2 cups of water and bring to a boil. Reduce heat and let simmer for 15 minutes. Let stand for 5 minutes or until thickened.

Beef Stroganoff

Beef Stroganoff

Bulk Batch Shopping List

Makes 10-11 quart-sized jars

Thrive Bechamel Sauce (2 pantry cans)
Thrive Espagnole Gravy (1 pantry can)
Sour Cream Powder (2 pantry cans)
Beef Bouillon (1 pantry cans)
FD Beef Slices (1 #10 can)
FD Mushrooms (1 pantry can)
Egg Noodle Pasta (25 cups)
Dill Weed

Ingredients per Jar:

Makes 4-5 servings per quart jar

1/2 c. Thrive Bechamel Sauce
2 T. Thrive Espagnole Gravy
1/2 c. Sour Cream Powder
2 T. Beef Bouillon
2 tsp. Dill Weed
1 c. FD Beef Slices
2 1/2 c. Egg Noodle Pasta (or favorite pasta)
1/3 c. FD Mushrooms

Directions:

To make jar: Add ingredients to jar in order listed for a prettier jar, add ingredients in reverse order if you want to do heaping servings. Add an oxygen absorber or seal with a Foodsaver jar lid attachment.

To prepare: In a large saucepan bring 5 ½ cups of water to a boil. Add contents of jar and let simmer for 15-20 minutes. Let stand for 5 minutes to thicken.

BEEF STROGANOFF

1/2 c. Thrive Bechamel Sauce
2 T. Thrive Espagnole Gravy
1/2 c. Sour Cream Powder
2 T. Beef Bouillon
2 tsp. Dill Weed
1 c. FD Beef Slices
2 1/2 c. Egg Noodle Pasta
1/3 c. FD Mushrooms

In a large saucepan bring 5 ½ cups of water to a boil. Add contents of jar and let simmer for 15-20 minutes. Let stand for 5 minutes to thicken.

http://mealsinajar.net

Beef Veggie Skillet

Beef Veggie Skillet

Bulk Batch Shopping List

Makes 10-11 quart-sized jars

Thrive Tomato Sauce Mix (1 pantry can)
FD Chopped Onions (1 pantry can)
FD Red Bell Peppers (2 pantry cans)
FD Zucchini (2 pantry cans)
FD Asparagus (2 pantry cans)
FD Ground Beef (1 #10 can)
FD Parmesan Cheese (1 pantry can)
Oregano
Minced Garlic
Cayenne Pepper
Ground Mustard
Salt

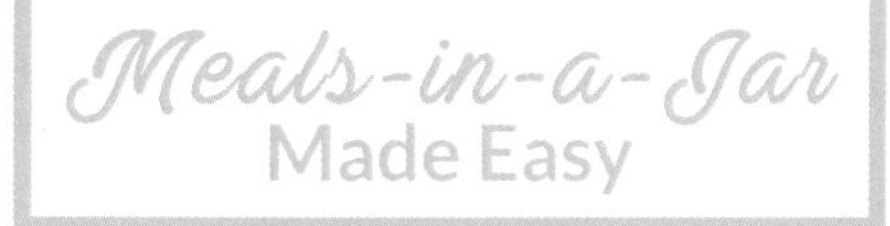

BEEF VEGGIE SKILLET

1 tsp. Minced Garlic
1 tsp. Salt
1/8 tsp. Cayenne Pepper
1/8 tsp. Dry Ground Mustard
1/2 tsp. Oregano
1/4 c. Thrive Tomato Sauce Mix
1/4 c. FD Chopped Onions
1/2 c. FD Red Bell Peppers
1/2 c. FD Zucchini
1/2 c. FD Asparagus
1 c. FD Ground Beef
Optional: 2 T. FD Parmesan Cheese

In a large skillet heat up 2 T. olive oil. Pour contents of the jar into the pan and stir. Gradually add 2 cups of water and stir. Cook for about 7-8 minutes until sauce is thickened. Sprinkle parmesan cheese over top if desired.

http://mealsinajar.net

Ingredients per Jar:

Makes 4-5 servings per quart jar

1 tsp. Minced Garlic
1 tsp. Salt
1/8 tsp. Cayenne Pepper
1/8 tsp. Dry Ground Mustard
1/2 tsp. Oregano
1/4 c. Thrive Tomato Sauce Mix
1/4 c. FD Chopped Onions
1 c. FD Ground Beef
1/2 c. FD Red Bell Peppers
1/2 c. FD Zucchini
1/2 c. FD Asparagus
2 T. FD Parmesan Cheese (optional - in baggie)

Directions:

To make jar: Add ingredients to jar in order listed for a prettier jar, add ingredients in reverse order if you want to do heaping servings. (Place parmesan cheese in separate baggie on top if desired) Add an oxygen absorber or seal with a Foodsaver jar lid attachment.

To prepare: In a large skillet heat up 2 T. olive oil. Pour contents of the jar into the pan and stir. Gradually add 2 cups of water and stir. Cook for about 7-8 minutes until sauce is thickened and beef is fully rehydrated. Sprinkle parmesan cheese over top if desired.

Cheeseburger Soup

Cheeseburger Soup

Bulk Batch Shopping List

Makes 10-11 quart-sized jars

Chicken Bouillon (1 pantry can)
Thrive Béchamel Sauce Mix (1 pantry can)
Instant Milk Powder (2 pantry cans)
Sour Cream Powder (1 pantry can)
Thrive Cheese Sauce (1 pantry can)
FD Chopped Onions (1 pantry can)
FD Sweet Corn (1 pantry can)
FD Celery (1 pantry can)
FD Cheddar Cheese (1 pantry can)
FD Potato Dices (1 #10 can)
FD Ground Beef (1 #10 can)
Spices/Seasonings

CHEESEBURGER SOUP

1 tsp. Basil
1 tsp. Parsley
1/4 tsp. Black Pepper
1 tsp. Seasoned Salt
2 tsp. Chicken Bouillon
1/4 c. Thrive Béchamel Sauce Mix
1/2 c. Instant Milk Powder
2 T. Sour Cream Powder
1/3 c. Thrive Cheese Sauce
2 T. FD Chopped Onions
1/4 c. FD Sweet Corn
1/4 c. FD Celery
1/3 c. FD Cheddar Cheese
3/4 c. FD Potato Dices
2/3 c. FD Ground Beef

Combine contents of jar with 6 cups of water and bring to a boil. Reduce heat and let simmer for 30 minutes.

http://mealsinajar.net

Ingredients per Jar:

Makes 4-5 servings per quart jar

1 tsp. Basil
1 tsp. Parsley
1/4 tsp. Black Pepper
1 tsp. Seasoned Salt
2 tsp. Chicken Bouillon
1/4 c. Thrive Béchamel Sauce Mix
1/2 c. Instant Milk Powder
2 T. Sour Cream Powder
1/3 c. Thrive Cheese Sauce
2 T. FD Chopped Onions
1/4 c. FD Sweet Corn
1/4 c. FD Celery
1/3 c. FD Cheddar Cheese
3/4 c. FD Potato Dices
2/3 c. FD Ground Beef

Directions:

To make jar: Add ingredients to jar in order listed for a prettier jar, add ingredients in reverse order if you want to do heaping servings. Add an oxygen absorber or seal with a Foodsaver jar lid attachment.

To prepare: Combine contents of jar with 6 cups of water and bring to a boil. Reduce heat and let simmer for 30 minutes.

Korean Beef

Korean Beef

Bulk Batch Shopping List

Makes 10-11 quart-sized jars

FD Chopped Onions (1 pantry can)
FD Green Peas (1 pantry can)
FD Red Bell Peppers (1 pantry can)
FD Broccoli (2 pantry cans)
FD Shredded Beef (1 #10 can)
Rice (24 cups)
Brown Sugar (5 cups)
Spices/Seasonings

KOREAN BEEF

1/3 c. Brown Sugar
1/2 T. Cornstarch
1/2 T. Ground Ginger
1/4 tsp. Crushed Red Pepper
1/2 T. Garlic Powder
1/4 tsp. Seasoned Salt
2 T. FD Chopped Onions
1/4 c. FD Green Peas
1/4 c. FD Red Bell Peppers
1/2 c. FD Broccoli
1 c. FD Shredded Beef

In a medium saucepan combine butter, water, and soy sauce. Pour in contents of jar and bring to a boil. Let simmer for 12-15 minutes or until fully refreshed. Serve over cooked rice.

http://mealsinajar.net

Ingredients per Jar:

Makes 4-5 servings per quart jar

1/3 c. Brown Sugar
1/2 T. Cornstarch
1/2 T. Ground Ginger
1/4 tsp. Crushed Red Pepper
1/2 T. Garlic Powder
1/4 tsp. Seasoned Salt
2 T. FD Chopped Onions
1/4 c. FD Green Peas
1/4 c. FD Red Bell Peppers
1/2 c. FD Broccoli
1 c. FD Shredded Beef

For Serving:
1 T. Butter
2 c. Water
1/3 c. Soy Sauce
2 c. Rice (cooked)

Directions:

To make jar: Add 1st 11 ingredients to jar in order listed for a prettier jar, add ingredients in reverse order if you want to do heaping servings. Measure out 2 cups of your favorite rice and put in a pint size jar and store with the jar. Add an oxygen absorber or seal with a Foodsaver jar lid attachment.

To prepare: In a medium saucepan combine butter, water, and soy sauce. Pour in contents of jar and bring to a boil. Let simmer for 12-15 minutes or until fully refreshed. Serve over cooked rice.

Kung Pao Beef

Kung Pao Beef

Bulk Batch Shopping List

Makes 10-11 quart-sized jars

FD Green Chili Peppers (1 pantry can)

FD Onion Slices (2 pantry cans)

FD Red Bell Peppers (2 pantry cans)

FD Green Bell Peppers (2 pantry cans)

FD Beef Dices (1 #10 can)

Peanuts (6 cups)

Minced Garlic

Ingredients per Jar:

Makes 4-5 servings per quart jar

2 tsp. Minced Garlic
1/4 c. FD Green Chili Peppers
1/2 c. FD Onion Slices
1/2 c. FD Red Bell Peppers
1/2 c. FD Green Bell Peppers
1 c. FD Beef Dices
1/2 c. Roasted Peanuts

For Sauce:
1/4 c. Soy Sauce
1 T. BBQ Sauce
1 T. Sesame Oil
1 T. White Sugar
1 T. Cornstarch
1/4 c. Water

2 T. Vegetable Oil
1 c. Water

Directions:

To make jar: Add 1st 6 ingredients into the jar in the order listed. Add a small baggie of peanuts or 1/2 cup of peanuts in a zip-lock bag to top of jar. Add an oxygen absorber or seal with a Foodsaver jar lid attachment.

To prepare: Put 2 T. vegetable oil into a frying pan. Add first 6 ingredients and saute for 1-2 minutes. Add 1 c. of water and allow to hydrate. Meanwhile combine sauce ingredients in small dish. Pour over beef mixture and add peanuts. Heat for 2-3 minutes until sauce is thickened.

KUNG PAO BEEF

2 tsp. Minced Garlic
1/4 c. FD Green Chili Peppers
1/2 c. FD Onion Slices
1/2 c. FD Red Bell Peppers
1/2 c. FD Green Bell Peppers
1 c. FD Beef Dices
1/2 c. Roasted Peanuts

1/4 c. Soy Sauce
1 T. BBQ Sauce
1 T. Sesame Oil
1 T. White Sugar
1 T. Cornstarch
1/4 c. Water

Put 2 T. vegetable oil into a frying pan. Add first 6 ingredients and saute for 1-2 minutes. Add 1 c. of water and allow to hydrate. Meanwhile combine remaining ingredients in small bowl to make sauce. Pour over beef mixture and add peanuts. Heat for 2-3 minutes until sauce is thickened.

http://mealsinajar.net

Philly Cheesesteak

Philly Cheesesteak

Bulk Batch Shopping List

Makes 10-11 quart-sized jars

FD Thrive Shredded Beef (1 #10 can)
FD Thrive Mozzarella Cheese (1 #10 can)
FD Green Bell Peppers (1 pantry can)
FD Mushrooms (1 pantry can)
FD Sliced Onions (2 pantry cans)
Thrive Espagnole Sauce (1 pantry can)
Seasoned Salt

Ingredients per Jar:

Makes 4-5 servings per quart jar

1 1/2 T. Thrive Espagnole Sauce
1 tsp. Seasoned Salt
1 c. FD Mozzarella Cheese
1/2 c. FD Sliced Onions
1/3 c. FD Green Bell Peppers
1/3 c. FD Mushrooms
1 c. FD Shredded Beef

Directions:

To make jar: Add ingredients to jar in order listed for a prettier jar, add ingredients in reverse order if you want to do heaping servings. Add an oxygen absorber or seal with a Foodsaver jar lid attachment.

To prepare: In a large saucepan bring 2 1/2 cups of water to a boil. Add contents of jar and let simmer for 5-10 minutes.

Serve on a hoagie bun, in a lettuce wrap, or eat plain as a stew.

PHILLY CHEESESTEAK

1 c. FD Shredded Beef
1 c. FD Mozzarella Cheese
1/3 c. FD Green Bell Peppers
1/3 c. FD Mushrooms
1/2 c. FD Sliced Onions
1 1/2 T. Thrive Espagnole Sauce
1 tsp. Seasoned Salt

In a large saucepan bring 2 1/2 cups of water to a boil. Add contents of jar and let simmer for 5-10 minutes.

Serve on a hoagie bun, in a lettuce wrap, or eat plain as a stew.

http://mealsinajar.net

Shepherd's Pie

Shepherd's Pie

Bulk Batch Shopping List

Makes 10-11 sets of jars

Thrive Tomato Sauce Mix (2 pantry cans)
Beef Bouillon (1 pantry can)
FD Chopped Onions (1 pantry can)
FD Sweet Corn (1 pantry can)
FD Small Diced Beef (1 #10 can)
Mashed Potato Flakes (2 #10 cans)
Instant Milk Powder (1 pantry can)
FD Cheddar Cheese (1 #10 can)
Minced Garlic
Italian Seasoning

SHEPHERD'S PIE

1/2 c. Thrive Tomato Sauce Mix
2 tsp. Italian Seasoning
1 tsp. Beef Bouillon
1 T. FD Garlic
2 T. FD Chopped Onions
1/3 c. FD Sweet Corn
1 c. FD Small Diced Beef

2 c. Mashed Potato Flakes
1/2 tsp. Salt
2 T. Instant Milk Powder
1 c. FD Cheddar Cheese (separate bag)

Combine contents of pint jar with 2 cups water in small pot. Simmer until thick. Pour into 8×8 baking dish. Bring 2 1/2 cups of water to boil. Add contents of quart jar (except cheese). Stir until smooth. Add over top of meat Refresh cheese and sprinkle on top. Bake at 350 degrees for 15 minutes.

http://mealsinajar.net

Ingredients per Jar:

Makes 4-5 servings per jar set

Jar 1 (pint):
1/2 c. Thrive Tomato Sauce Mix
2 tsp. Italian Seasoning
1 tsp. Beef Bouillon
1 T. Minced Garlic
2 T. FD Chopped Onions
1/3 c. FD Sweet Corn
1 c. FD Small Diced Beef

Jar 2 (quart):
2 c. Mashed Potato Flakes
1/2 tsp. Salt
2 T. Instant Milk Powder
1 c. FD Cheddar Cheese (separate bag)

Directions:

To make jars In jar 1, add 1st 7 ingredients to jar in order listed. In jar 2, add 1st 3 ingredients to jar. Pour cheese into a separate baggie and add to the top of the jar. Add an oxygen absorber to each jar or seal both jars with a Foodsaver jar lid attachment

To prepare: Combine contents of pint jar with 2 cups of water in small pot. Simmer until thickened. Pour into 8×8 baking dish. In separate pot, bring 2 1/2 cups of water to a boil, add contents of quart jar (except cheese). Stir well until smooth. Add potatoes over top of the meat mixture. Refresh cheese in separate container and sprinkle on top of potatoes. Bake at 350 degrees for 15 minutes.

Unstuffed Peppers

Unstuffed Peppers

Bulk Batch Shopping List

Makes 10-11 quart-sized jars

FD Ground Beef (2 pantry cans)
FD Chopped Onions (1 pantry can)
FD Green Bell Peppers (1 #10 can)
FD Red Bell Peppers (1 #10 can)
Tomato Powder (1 pantry can)
Beef Bouillon (1 pantry can)
Instant White Rice (11 cups)
Italian Seasoning
Minced Garlic
Seasoned Salt

UNSTUFFED PEPPERS

1/2 c. FD Ground Beef
1/4 c. FD Chopped Onions
1 c. FD Green Bell Peppers
1 c. FD Red Bell Peppers
1/4 c. Tomato Powder
1 c. Instant White Rice
1 T. Italian Seasoning
1/2 tsp. Seasoned Salt
2 tsp. FD Minced Garlic
2 T. Beef Bouillon

In a large saucepan bring 6 cups of water to a boil. Add contents of jar and let simmer for 15-20 minutes. For a thicker casserole meal use 4 cups. Sprinkle with cheddar cheese and serve.

http://mealsinajar.net

Ingredients per Jar:

Makes 4-5 servings per quart jar

2 tsp. Minced Garlic
1 T. Italian Seasoning
1/2 tsp. Seasoned Salt
1/4 c. Tomato Powder
2 T. Beef Bouillon
1/4 c. FD Chopped Onions
1 c. Instant White Rice
1/2 c. FD Ground Beef
1 c. FD Green Bell Peppers
1 c. FD Red Bell Peppers

Directions:

To make jar: Add ingredients to jar in order listed for a prettier jar, add ingredients in reverse order if you want to do heaping servings. Add an oxygen absorber or seal with a Foodsaver jar lid attachment.

To prepare: In a large saucepan bring 6 cups of water to a boil. Add contents of jar and let simmer for 15-20 minutes. For a thicker casserole meal use 4 cups. Top with cheddar cheese if desired and serve.

Veggie Beef Stew

Veggie Beef Stew

Bulk Batch Shopping List

Makes 10-11 quart-sized jars

Thrive Espagnole Gravy (1 pantry can)
Beef Bouillon (1 pantry can)
FD Chopped Onions (1 pantry can)
Dehydrated Carrot Dices (1 pantry can)
FD Celery (2 pantry cans)
FD Green Peas (2 pantry cans)
Dehydrated Potato Chunks (1 #10 can)
FD Beef Slices (1 #10 can)
Pearled Barley (2 1/2 cups)
Seasoned Salt

VEGGIE BEEF STEW

1/3 c. Thrive Espagnole Gravy
1 T. Beef Bouillon
1 tsp. Seasoned Salt
1/4 c. Pearled Barley
3 T. FD Chopped Onions
2 T. Deyhdrated Carrot Dices
1/2 c. FD Celery
1/2 c. FD Green Peas
3/4 c. Dehydrated Potato Chunks
1 c. FD Beef Slices

In a large saucepan bring 7 cups of water to a boil. Add contents of jar and let simmer for 40 minutes or until barley and potatoes are soft. Stir occasionally.

Serving Tip: Add salt and pepper to taste, serve with your favorite biscuits or rolls.

http://mealsinajar.net

Ingredients per Jar:

Makes 4-6 servings per quart jar

1/3 c. Thrive Espagnole Gravy
1 T. Beef Bouillon
1 tsp. Seasoned Salt
1/4 c. Pearled Barley
3 T. FD Chopped Onions
2 T. Dehydrated Carrot Dices
1/2 c. FD Celery
1/2 c. FD Green Peas
3/4 c. Dehydrated Potato Chunks
1 c. FD Beef Slices

Directions:

To make jar: Add ingredients to jar in order listed for a prettier jar, add ingredients in reverse order if you want to do heaping servings. Add an oxygen absorber or seal with a Foodsaver jar lid attachment.

To prepare: In a large saucepan bring 7 cups of water to a boil. Add contents of jar and let simmer for 40 minutes or until barley and potatoes are soft. Stir occasionally. Add salt and pepper to taste, serve with your favorite biscuits or rolls.

Dinner is essential to life. Therefore, make it good!

MAIN COURSES: NO MEAT

Cheesy Corn Chowder

Cheesy Corn Chowder

Bulk Batch Shopping List

Makes 11-12 quart-sized jars

Instant Milk Powder (1 pantry can)

FD Green Onions (1 pantry can)

FD Cheddar Cheese (1 #10 can)

FD Sweet Corn (2 #10 cans)

FD Red Bell Peppers (2 pantry cans)

Chicken Bouillon (1 pantry can)

Ground Pepper

Salt

Ingredients per Jar:

Makes 3-4 servings per quart jar

1/4 tsp. Ground Pepper
1/2 tsp. Salt
2 tsp. Chicken Bouillon
2 T. Instant Milk Powder
1/4 c. FD Green Onions
3/4 c. FD Cheddar Cheese
2 c. FD Sweet Corn
1/2 c. FD Red Bell Peppers

Directions:

To make jar: Add ingredients to jar in order listed for a prettier jar, add ingredients in reverse order if you want to do heaping servings. Add an oxygen absorber or seal with a Foodsaver jar lid attachment.

To prepare: Mix contents of jar with 3 cups of water in a large saucepan. Bring to a boil then reduce heat and simmer for 5-7 minutes. Blend the soup with an immersion blender until desired consistency is reached. You can also put about half of it in the blender until smooth and then return to the pot and stir.

CHEESY CORN CHOWDER

1/4 tsp. Ground Pepper
1/2 tsp. Salt
2 tsp. Chicken Bouillon
2 T. Instant Milk Powder
1/4 c. FD Green Onions
3/4 c. FD Cheddar Cheese
2 c. FD Sweet Corn
1/2 c. FD Red Bell Peppers

Mix contents of jar with 3 cups of water in a large saucepan. Bring to a boil then reduce heat and simmer for 5-7 minutes. Blend the soup with an immersion blender until desired consistency is reached. You can also put about half of it in the blender until smooth and then return to the pot and stir.

http://mealsinajar.net

Life is short,
eat dessert first

DRINKS / DESSERTS

Christmas Cookies

Christmas Cookies

Bulk Batch Shopping List

Makes 10-11 quart-sized jars

FD Cranberries (1 #10 can)

Dried Egg Powder (1 pantry can)

White Chocolate Chips (11 cups)

Quick Oats (11 cups)

White Flour (9 cups)

White Sugar (4 cups)

Brown Sugar (4 cups)

Vanilla Powder

Baking Powder

Baking Soda

Salt

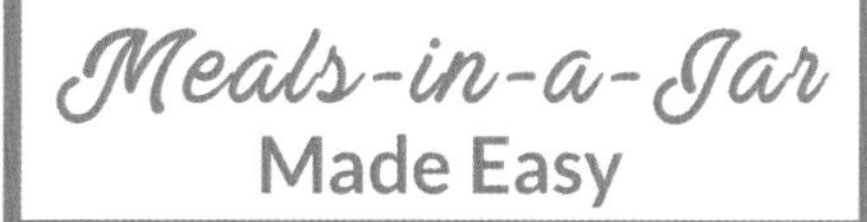

CHRISTMAS COOKIES

1/3 c. White Sugar
1/3 . Brown Sugar, packed
1 T. Dried Egg Powder
3/4 c. White Flour
1 tsp. Vanilla Powder
1/2 tsp. Baking Powder
1/8 tsp. Baking Soda
1/8 tsp. Salt
1 c. Quick Oats
1 c. FD Cranberries or Craisins
1 c. White Chocolate Chips
1/2 c. butter, melted
2 T. water

Stir up contents of jar in a large bowl. Beat in melted butter and water. Cover and refrigerate for 30 min. Drop by spoonfuls on an ungreased baking sheet. Bake at 375° for 8-10 minutes or until browned. Cool on wire racks.

http://mealsinajar.net

Ingredients per Jar:

Makes approximagely 24 cookies per quart jar

1/3 c. White Sugar
1/3 . Brown Sugar, packed
1 T. Dried Egg Powder
3/4 c. White Flour
1 tsp. Vanilla Powder
1/2 tsp. Baking Powder
1/8 tsp. Baking Soda
1/8 tsp. Salt
1 c. Quick Oats
1 c. FD Cranberries or Craisins
1 c. White Chocolate Chips

For Cooking:
1/2 c. butter, melted
2 T. water

Directions:

To make jar: Add ingredients to jar in order listed. Add an oxygen absorber or seal with a Foodsaver jar lid attachment.

To prepare: Stir up contents of jar in a large bowl. Beat in melted butter and water. Cover and refrigerate for 30 min. Drop by spoonfuls on an ungreased baking sheet. Bake at 375° for 8-10 minutes or until browned. Cool on wire racks.

Easy Wassail

Easy Wassail

Bulk Batch Shopping List

Makes 10-11 pint-sized jars

FD Fuji Apples (2 family cans)
Lemonade Powder (1 pantry can)
Tang Drink Mix (1 1/2 cups)
Brown Sugar (1 1/2 cups)
Whole Cinnamon Sticks (22 sticks)
Ground Ginger
Ground Nutmeg
Whole Cloves

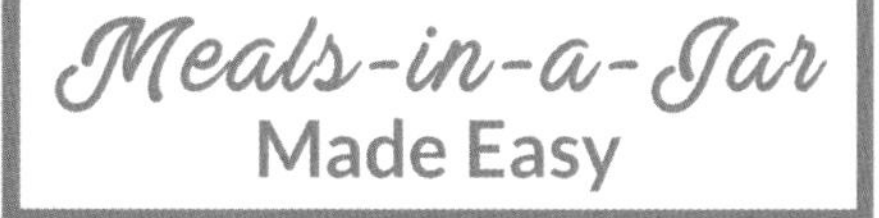

EASY WASSAIL

1 c. FD Fuji Apples, powdered
2 T. Tang Drink Mix
1/8 tsp. Ground Ginger
1/8 tsp. Ground Nutmeg
1/16 tsp. Lemonade Powder
3 T. Brown Sugar
2 Whole Cinnamon Sticks
8 Whole Cloves
1 c. FD Fuji Apple Slices

In a medium stock pot combine 5 cups of water with contents of jar. Using medium low heat bring to a simmer. Simmer 30-40 minutes. Remove apples and whole cloves. Add additional brown sugar to taste if desired. Ladle into mugs and enjoy!

http://mealsinajar.net

Ingredients per Jar:

Makes 4-6 servings per pint jar

1 c. FD Fuji Apples, powdered
2 T. Tang Drink Mix
1/8 tsp. Ground Ginger
1/8 tsp. Ground Nutmeg
1/16 tsp. Lemonade Powder
3 T. Brown Sugar
2 Whole Cinnamon Sticks
8 Whole Cloves
1 c. FD Fuji Apple Slices

Directions:

To make jar: Place ingredients into the jar in the order listed. Place apple slices in and around the cinnamon sticks to make it look pretty. You can fill the rest of the jar with apples if there is room to spare after 1 cup.

To prepare: In a medium stock pot combine 5 cups of water with contents of jar. Using medium low heat bring to a simmer. Simmer 30-40 minutes. Remove apples and whole cloves. Add additional brown sugar to taste if desired. Ladle into mugs and enjoy!

Fruit Galette

Fruit Galette

Bulk Batch Shopping List

Makes 10-11 quart-sized jars

FD Peaches (1 #10 can)

FD Strawberries (2 pantry cans)

FD Blueberries (1 pantry)

Butter Powder (1 pantry can)

All-Purpose Flour (13 cups)

White Sugar (5 cups)

Kosher Salt

Cornstarch

Cinnamon

Ingredients per Jar:

Makes 1 galette with 2-3 servings per quart jar

Bag 1:
3/4 c. White Flour
1/2 tsp. Kosher Salt
1/2 T. White Sugar
1/3 c. Butter Powder

Bag 2:
1/2 c. White Flour

Bag 3:
1/4 c. White Sugar
1/2 T. Cornstarch
1/4 tsp. Cinnamon

Jar:
1 c. FD Peaches
1/2 c. FD Strawberries
1/4 c. FD Blueberries

Directions:

To make jar: Combine the ingredients into small sealable bags. Label each bag with a 1, 2, or 3. Place bags in the bottom of a wide-mouth jar. Add peaches, strawberries, and blueberries.

To prepare: Pour fruit into a medium bowl and remove bags from jar. Refresh fruit in 1/2 c. of water. Put Bag 1 into food processor and pulse to mix. Add 1/3 c of ice water. Pulse until dough is clumpy. Add Bag 2. Pulse until dough is grainy. Place dough in medium bowl. Mix in 1 T. of water at a time (3-4 total) until dough holds together when pinched. Roll dough into a 10" circle. Place on parchment paper-lined cookie sheet. Mix Bag 3 into fruit and place in the center of crust. Fold the edges and pinch. Brush edges with milk and sprinkle with sugar if desired. Bake for 25-30 minutes at 400 degrees.

Meals-in-a-Jar
Made Easy

FRUIT GALETTE

1 1/2 c. White Flour, separated
1/2 tsp. Kosher Salt
3/4 c. White Sugar, separated
1/3 c. Butter Powder
1/2 T. Cornstarch
1/4 tsp. Cinnamon
1 c. FD Peaches
1/2 c. FD Strawberries
1/4 c. FD Blueberries

Pour fruit into a medium bowl and remove bags from jar. Refresh fruit in 1/2 c. of water. Put Bag 1 into food processor and pulse to mix. Add 1/3 c of ice water. Pulse until dough is clumpy. Add Bag 2. Pulse until dough is grainy. Place dough in medium bowl. Mix in 1 T. of water at a time (3-4 total) until dough holds together when pinched. Roll dough into a 10" circle. Place on parchment paper-lined cookie sheet. Mix Bag 3 into fruit and place in the center of crust. Fold the edges and pinch. Brush edges with milk and sprinkle with sugar if desired. Bake for 25-30 minutes at 400 degrees.

http://mealsinajar.net

You can never have too many "kitchen" tools in your toolbox

APPENDIX: BONUSES

Meals-in-a-Jar Calculator

I created a meal-in-a-jar calculator to help price the jars I use in local Thrive Life classes I teach. We get together in groups to make a big batch of meals and each person goes home with a few. This calculator is a bonus that you can use and customize to your liking. It has the serving sizes and prices based on Thrive Life products but is pretty easy to swap out for whatever brand and sizes you are using. Please feel free to email me at info@foodstoragemadeeasy.net if you have any issues or problems using the calculator.

Editing the calculator: "Cost per can" is an easy column to edit. Simply type in the price of the can that you purchased. The column highlighted in blue is where all the magic happens in this calculator. If the food you are buying comes in a different size can (for example you bought a pantry can instead of a #10 can) you will need to adjust it. You also may need to adjust it if the serving size on your can is different. I generally keep the units in cups but for some items that just doesn't make sense. Double-click on the blue column to see a formula that looks like this =ROUNDUP((B9*B5)/10,0) You will simply need to swap the red number for the number of servings per can. Then the calculator will round up to the "Total # of cans" you should buy.

You can experiment with the "# of jars" you are making to get the most cost-effective price per jar. If you are only making a few at a time you can plan on having extra of most items.

THRIVE LIFE MEAL-IN-A-JAR CALCULATOR

Last Updated July 2022

Prices based on 10 cups per #10 can and 3.5 cups per Pantry Can at "Delivery" Prices

How many meals in a jar are you making?			Cost Per Jar		$ -			Total Product Cost	$ -
Ingredient	**Quantity**	**Unit**	**Cost Per Unit**		**Cost Per Jar**	**Total # of cans (rounded up)**		**Cost per can**	**Total Cost**
FRUITS									
Apples, Fuji (FD)		Cup	$ 3.65	Cup	$ -	0	#10 cans	$36.54	$ -
Apples, Granny Smith (FD) - *Limited Time*		Cup	$ 3.37	Cup	$ -	0	#10 cans	$33.65	$ -
Applesauce - *Limited Time*		1/4 Cup	$ 1.57	1/4 Cup	$ -	0	#10 cans	$62.81	$ -
Apricots (FD) - *Limited Time*		Cup	$ 5.46	Cup	$ -	0	#10 cans	$54.56	$ -
Banana Slices (FD)		Cup	$ 3.67	Cup	$ -	0	#10 cans	$36.71	$ -
Blackberries (FD)		Cup	$ 5.01	Cup	$ -	0	#10 cans	$50.14	$ -
Blueberries (FD)		Cup	$ 5.07	Cup	$ -	0	#10 cans	$50.65	$ -
Grapes, Red Seedless (FD)		Cup	$ 6.49	Cup	$ -	0	#10 cans	$64.93	$ -
Mangoes (FD)		Cup	$ 4.63	Cup	$ -	0	#10 cans	$46.32	$ -
Peach Slices (FD)		Cup	$ 5.09	Cup	$ -	0	#10 cans	$50.91	$ -
Pineapple (FD)		Cup	$ 4.95	Cup	$ -	0	#10 cans	$49.46	$ -
Raspberries (FD)		Cup	$ 4.61	Cup	$ -	0	#10 cans	$46.06	$ -
Strawberries, Sliced (FD)		Cup	$ 3.89	Cup	$ -	0	#10 cans	$38.92	$ -
Sweet Cherries (FD) - *Limited Time*		Cup	$ 7.18	Cup	$ -	0	#10 cans	$71.82	$ -

DOWNLOAD CALCULATOR AT http://bit.ly/MIJ-calc

Jar Labels

I have created downloadable jar labels for every recipe in this book! You can take these to a print shop or print them on your home printer. You can print them on sticker paper to stick directly on jars, or just tape them on with double-sided tape. There are 6 recipes per page so you can use them to make bulk batches of each meal or have spares when one wears out.

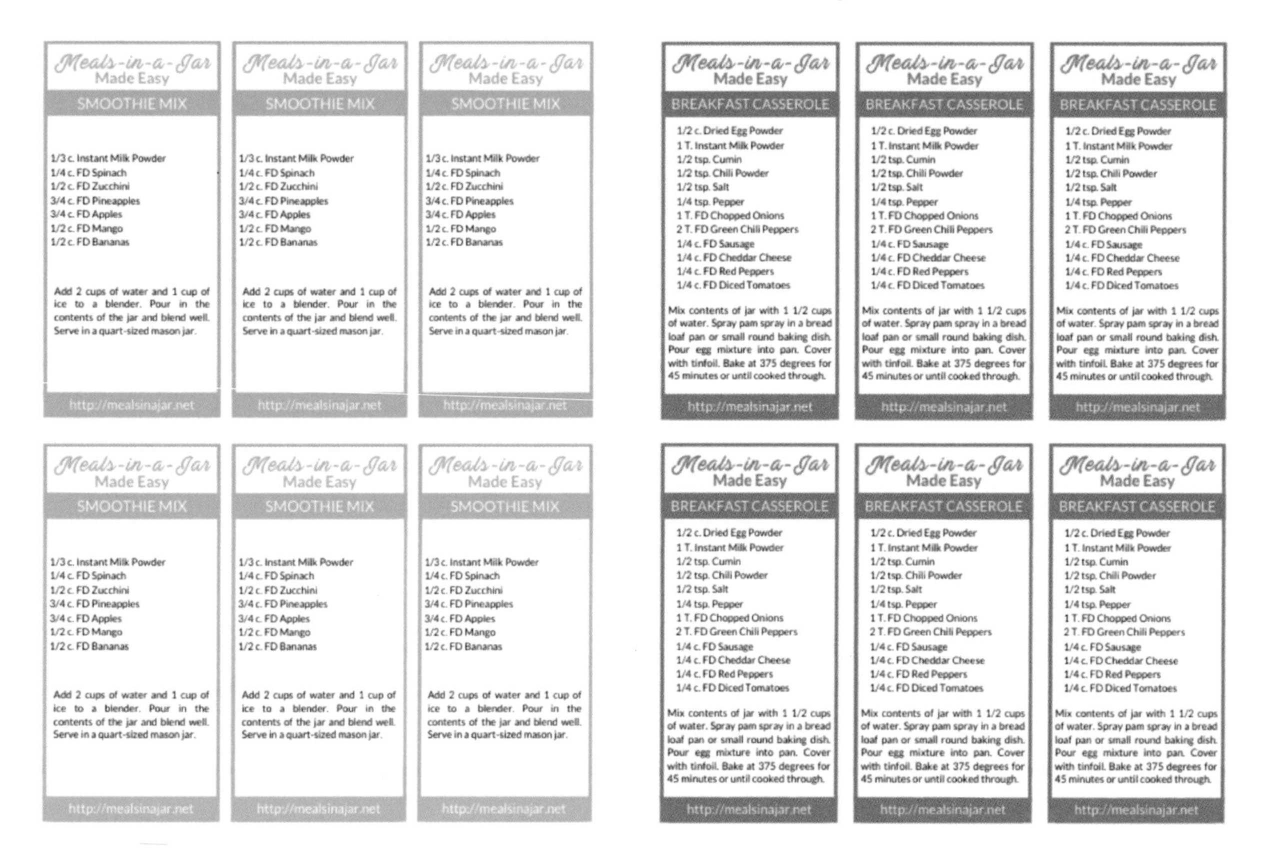

DOWNLOAD ALL JAR LABELS AT http://bit.ly/MIJ-labels

Monthly Recipe Emails / Texts / Facebook Group

Every month I take the monthly specials from **Thrive Life** and create a new recipe based around what's on sale. If you would like to receive notification of new recipes as they come out you can get access to them using one of these methods:

- Join the Facebook community at *https://www.facebook.com/groups/monthlymealsinajar*
- Subscribe via text message by texting "*MIJ*" *to* ***717-788-3663***
- Subscribe via email at *https://bit.ly/MIJ-emails*

If you already receive my monthly emails you will notice they will now begin to follow the same format and style of the book recipes so you will have consistency if you use the new recipes in the future.

If you aren't already ordering freeze-dried foods from Thrive Life, don't forget to use my link at http://jodiandjulie.thrivelife.com when you shop. Thank you so much!

RECIPE INDEX

Check out these other books co-authored by Jodi Weiss Schroeder:

Food Storage Made Easy

by Julie Weiss and Jodi Weiss Schroeder (formerly Jodi Moore)

A complete guide to planning, buying, and using your food storage using 10 simple BabySteps.

This 3-part program consists of the following parts:

- BabyStep Checklists: Gives specific food storage or preparedness items to buy every 2 weeks for you to learn about and to try cooking with.
- Food Storage Encyclopedia: Contains detailed information about every aspect of your food storage and emergency preparedness plans which we discuss in the checklists.
- Recipe Appendix: 60+ recipes to help you use all of the foods from the checklists plus measurement equivalents and substitution charts.

Available on Amazon at https://amzn.to/3PenWy4

Meals in Minutes

by Tracy Taylor, Christina Riostirado, Jodi Weiss Schroeder

100+ recipes featuring Thrive Life freeze-dried foods put together by three veteran consultants.

This book takes all the guesswork out of cooking with freeze-dried food. We want to encourage people to open their cans and discovered how much time and money you can save in the kitchen creating delicious and EASY recipes for your family.

Available on Amazon at https://amzn.to/3HluSaE

Made in United States
Orlando, FL
22 September 2024